Weaving and the Construction of Woven Fabrics

By

Richard Marsden

WEAVING AND THE CONSTRUCTION OF WOVEN FABRICS.

The principles of weaving.—Its simplest form.—The variety of weaves.—Texture of plain cloth.—Healds and reed.—Weaving with one shaft of healds.—Ornamentation of plain cloth.—*The plain weave*, and its variations.—*The three-shaft twill;* designs and drafts.—*The four-shaft twill;* designs and drafts.—*The five-shaft twill;* designs, etc.—*The six-shaft twill;* designs, weave plans, and drafts.—*The seven-shaft twill;* designs and weave plans.—*The eight-shaft twill*, and variations.—*The nine-shaft twill.*—*The ten-shaft twill*, etc.—*Double and multiple cloth weaving;* description.—The fundamental principles of double-cloth weaving; numerous illustrations.—The laying out of fancy double cloths.—*Crimped cloths;* how to get the best effects; illustrations.—*Gauze or Leno weaving;* description.—Best expression of the gauze weave.—Light and elaborate effects.—*Cords, velvets, velveteens, plushes, moleskins;* descriptions and illustrations.—*Jacquard harness;* the London and Norwich ties.—The hooks of the jacquard machine.—Building the harness.—*Damask weaving;* the shedding capacity of the jacquard machine.—Designing for the jacquard.—Design or point paper.—Simplicity of jacquard drafts.—"Casting out" hooks and mails.—*The analysis or dissection of woven fabrics;* points to be noted, and method of procedure.

THE principles of an art may be called its foundation stones; and the natural consecutive developments from them the successive courses of the building contributing to the formation of the structure that, in its finished state, becomes a thing of utility, beauty, and a joy for ever. Some people may regard this as exaggerated language to apply to the somewhat homely and prosaic art of weaving, as they are accustomed to regard it. But such opinions, where they exist, may safely be attributed to an imperfectly developed capacity of observation, rather than to the absence or deficiency of beauty in the thing observed, when that is the art of weaving. The primary object of the art is the provision of raiment for mankind, and for use in their dwellings. The fabrics devoted to these purposes may be plain, or be slightly or elaborately decorated. These, in their corresponding degree, call into requisition the simple, medium, or the most complex principles and mechanism of the art in order to produce the desired results. This chapter will, therefore, be devoted to an attempt to expound these principles, leaving the mechanism for subsequent review.

The writer has already, in a previous chapter, defined weaving as "the art of arranging, at right angles to each other, two or more series of threads of any suitable material, and binding them together by passing each thread under and over, and sometimes partially around, one another in regular alternation, or in such other order as may be needed to produce the required effect, by which arrangement they assume and retain an expanded form, rendering the fabric adaptable to many uses."

This definition might very properly be enlarged as not being sufficiently inclusive, as it does not bring in several classes of textile fabrics that can be made from a single thread. As instances of these we may point out knitted fabrics, nets, and point lace. Besides these, of which some people may doubt the appropriateness of the classification when brought within the category of textile fabrics, it is possible, and not only possible but a common practice to make fabrics in this manner from single threads. When in the production of these classes of fabrics the number of threads is increased, as they may be in knitting, netting, and the making of pillow lace, it is usually done to facilitate production, or to obtain a greater variety of results. As, however, it is not within the purpose of this work to give an exposition of these phases of the textile arts, but of the principles of weaving as ordinarily understood, they will not require more than a very slight reference.

In the interests of textile students, however, before leaving this point, we may observe that a properly woven fabric as ordinarily understood, and including warp and weft, may be made from one single thread. As an experiment to prove this, let the student take a needle and a length of cotton thread, and, using it singly, pass it backward and forward, say through two pieces of paper kept an inch apart, for about twenty times, placing the thread at each passage alongside and parallel with the one put in before. This will give forty warp threads. Next turn the needle to the side of these, and pass it under and over each thread in succession until the needle passes out at the opposite side, drawing the thread close up. This done, reverse its direction, and alternate the interlacing until it emerges near where it first entered. Repeat this process until the thread in the needle is used up, or the warp threads are filled. In both cases take care that the threads are placed parallel and close together. It will then be seen that a perfect piece of cloth has thus been made, and if done skilfully it would not be easy for other than experts to say that it had not been produced by ordinary appliances. This is the irreducible simplicity of weaving, and as thus described is often used to effect repairs to fine linens and other fine fabrics in Germany, where the women are exceedingly skilful in such work. In England it is occasionally seen in the woollen districts, and in humble homes resort is had to it for mending hosiery, when it is familiarly known as "darning." With these observations on the elementary principle we may proceed to a more methodical exposition of the subject.

Weaving is the name given to the art of constructing textile fabrics. It is of the most simple, or the most elaborately complex character, according to the requirements of the articles sought to be made. The simplest form, as ordinarily understood and practised, requires the employment of two series of threads only. These are respectively termed the warp and the weft, or, as the latter is sometimes termed, the woof. The last name, however, is an archaic form of the word. The warp consists of the longitudinal threads, or those which extend in the direction of its greatest length. The weft threads are the transverse ones, or those that pass under and over the warp threads from side to side. The warp threads may be of any length according to requirement or convenience; the requirement being that they shall not be less than is necessary to make the piece of cloth long enough for use for its intended purpose; and the convenience being that they shall not be longer than in the aggregate form of the warp can be conveniently handled or dealt with in the process of weaving. The minimum length of the weft threads is that required to go across the warp. In practice, however, they are always much longer, being formed into pirns, placed into shuttles as large as can conveniently be used, and so drawn off and left in the warp as the shuttle makes its rapid successive passages. Thus in the cotton trade each warp thread may be anywhere in length from 500 to 1,500 yards or even more; and each weft thread from 200 to 1,000 yards or more, according to the fineness of the counts being used, or the capacity of the shuttle to carry it.

If the almost countless methods and combinations of methods now in vogue in weaving be carefully analyzed they will be found capable of being reduced to a very small number of weaves. The following are the principal:—plain, twill, satin, spot, flush, cross-warp, and double-cloth textures. These each and all give their own simple results, and by combination they can be made to yield an almost infinite variety of complex ones. Simple and complex are alike obtained by the variations in the order by which the threads of the warp are lifted and depressed for the reception of the weft. This action is the shedding process, and correspondingly the means employed to produce the effects rise from the most simple to the elaborately complex shedding power of the modern Jacquard machine. The fact also ought to be noted here that this capacity for producing variety is enormously increased when allied to the power given by the use of the system of multiple shuttle boxes of either the rising or revolving order.

The plain texture may be regarded as the foundation of all others, and therefore first calls for description. Let the student obtain and examine a piece of common calico, the coarser the better for his purpose, only taking care to obtain it of the full width. Examination will show it to consist of two series of threads, longitudinal and transverse ones. It will be observed that the warp threads lie parallel to each other in a common plane. The weft threads, it will be seen, intersect those of the warp, passing under and over them in alternating succession. Fig. 23 shows this construction plainly, the vertical threads, A, B, being warp threads, and the horizontal threads 1, 2 being weft threads. The detached portion of the figure at the top is a section, enlarged a little to show the construction clearly.

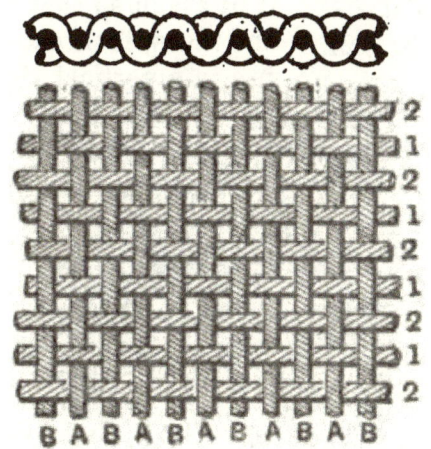

FIG. 23.

The student's sample will show the manner in which the weft threads are returned at the edges, the cloth making what is termed the selvage. In the actual process of construction the warp threads are maintained in a more or less tense condition, so that they are taken into the web of the cloth apparently in a straight line. But this is not actually so, as there is always more or less deflection into a more or less waved form, according to the thickness of the weft thread being inserted, and the degree of tension upon the warp. A similar deflection occurs in the weft threads, and when

COTTON WEAVING.

the giving way in this respect is mutual and about equal, the two series of threads are bedded together in the best manner. At the option of the weaver, and according to requirement, this flexure may be thrown into either the warp or weft threads. In the section given in the figure it is shown in the weft threads.

FIG. 24.

The design of this plain weave cloth, placed upon what is termed "point" or design paper, would appear very much like the squares of a chess-board. It is shown in fig. 24. Let it be assumed that the warp threads are white, and the weft threads black, and that the former run in a vertical direction, and the latter in a horizontal one. In the intersection of the threads which this represents the white squares show where a warp thread is uppermost, and the black squares where the weft

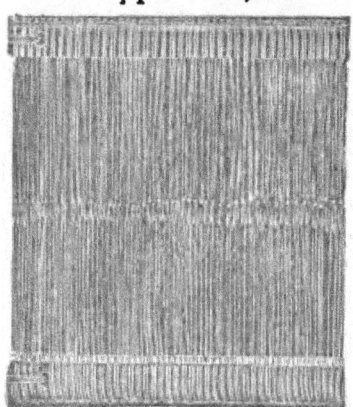 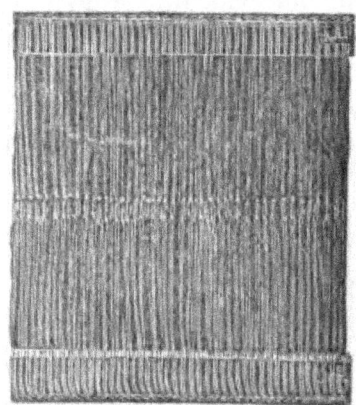

FIG. 25.—SHAFT OF HEALDS (BROKEN).

thread is on the top, and the warp thread down. The order of this alternation shows a plain weave, in silk weaving called a "tabby."

To obtain this result the weaver requires to have a certain control or command over the threads of the warp, in order to depress or elevate them in the manner required. This he gets in his shedding apparatus, the immediate instrument in this case being the heald, into which the warp threads are drawn.

The heald or heddle is composed of a cord formed of several strands of cotton, worsted, linen, or silk, but those used in the cotton trade are now in the main made of cotton, though still occasionally of worsted. A shaft of healds is shown in fig. 25, and a section of a set for weaving plain cloth in fig. 26. Healds are made upon a beautiful automatic machine exceedingly ingenious in construction, but space for a description here is not available. The eye in the centre, and through which the warp thread is drawn, is knitted into it when being made. The eye is formed of what is termed a mail, which may be made of steel, brass, or glass. The knitted eye is, however, the form in almost universal use in the cotton trade. These healds are mounted upon and stretched between two wooden laths, as shown in fig. 25, to the number of from 200 to 700, or more, according to the fineness or width of the cloth to be

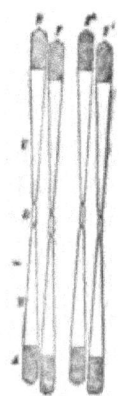

FIG. 26.

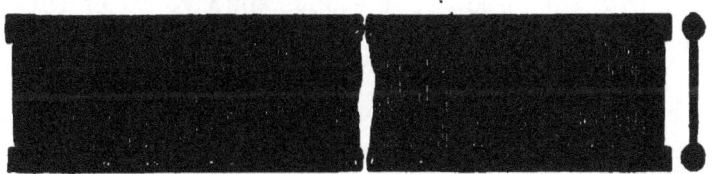

FIG. 27.—REED.   SECTION.

woven. So mounted they form a leaf or shaft of healds or heddles, and a number of these, from two to ten, or even more, constitute a set of healds, the number of shafts varying according to the character of the weave intended to be employed. Two are all that are really required for a plain weave, but owing to the greater facility obtained in the way of condensing the warp, or bringing its threads together, and minimizing friction upon the warp when being woven, four are generally used. Fig. 26 shows this arrangement. The two front leaves ascend and descend in the shedding together, and the two back ones in a similar manner alternate with them; that is, when the front ones are up the back ones are down, and *vice versâ*. The draft or order in which the threads are entered into the healds is as follows, reckoning from the front or the shaft of healds nearest the reed of the loom, and commencing on the left-hand side of the healds :— the first thread is drawn in the heald on the first shaft, and the second thread upon one in the third shaft; these two threads go together into the first dent or space in the reed ; the third thread is taken into the first heald on the second shaft, and the fourth thread into the first on the fourth shaft. This order is repeated and continued with the remaining portion of the warp until it is all drawn in. It is usual, however, in commencing the draft to draw two threads through each heald instead of one, for the first dozen healds or so, and to finish off in the same way. These double threads are called selvage threads, properly self-edge threads, and are purposely made stronger by doubling to resist the drag of the weft upon them, as it is returned into the shed. Sometimes the two outer threads are made threefold, and again, in very good fabrics, special selvage threads are introduced of twofold twisted yarns.

At this point it will be appropriate to describe in a very brief manner the reed, the ever-present adjunct of the healds. It is so named from having been originally composed of split reeds, the vegetable product of that name. It is now made of iron or brass, but mostly of the former. Wire of the required gauge is rolled and flattened to proper dimensions, highly polished, and run on a reel. It is then transferred to a reed-making machine, another of the wonderfully ingenious machines, adjuncts of the textile trades. The reed machine is furnished with the parts of the reed termed the reed back, composed of two strips of wood each for the top and the bottom. The machine is also supplied with two reels of pitch twine. Being set in operation, a strong or terminal dent is first put in, when the machine begins to cut the flattened wire into short lengths, and to place them successively in position with their ends between the two pairs of strips forming the backs. When one of these short lengths, or dents, as they are called, has been pushed forward, it is immediately secured in position by the machine wrapping a turn of the pitch-band close up to it around the two strips. Another strip is then advanced and the operation repeated, and so on until the reed is made of the required length. It is then finished off with another strong and broad dent. Fig. 27 gives an illustration of a front view and section. The more openly these dents are set in the reed the coarser or lower are its counts; and the closer they are the finer it becomes. This is all that is necessary to state in this place regarding it. The remainder will be more properly told in another section.

Before leaving this point, we may observe that since writing the above, the author has been informed by a textile expert that, in his young days, when on a visit to Ireland, he saw the rough frieze being woven with a single shaft of healds. This is a fact that will be interesting to the student, as it singularly and most remarkably confirms the theoretic elucidation of the progress of invention in the art of weaving given in Chapter I., pages 26 and 27. It would be highly interesting to learn whether this primitive method is still anywhere followed in Ireland.

It must not be assumed that ornamentation cannot be put into a plain weave cloth. There are several methods of effecting this. The first is by making what are called tape stripes parallel with its length. These are made by drawing-in the warp in double threads similar to the manner of the selvage threads, and doing this according to any given design. Many fabrics are made in this way, though not so many now as was once the case. Sometimes the effect is obtained by the use of two counts of yarn in the warp, fine and coarse, the latter to form the tape. Another variation can be introduced by using two counts of wefts and a two-shuttle loom. In this case a cord weft is introduced for a few picks at regular distances, making a stripe across the cloth. The first-described are termed "stripes," really parallel stripes; the latter are called "cross-over stripes," to distinguish them from those parallel. A further variation is obtained by the employment of these two methods in combination. This produces a class of fabrics termed "tape-checks." A great variety of these can be made, and formerly they were a very popular fabric. Another line of variation is obtained by the introduction of cords, as seen in the familiar instance of handkerchief borders.

It will be obvious that many other combinations and variations in ornamentation can be made by the introduction of coloured yarns in the warp and in the weft and in both. These need not be further enlarged upon, as an almost endless number will suggest themselves. The whole class of ginghams are types belonging to this division.

The Plain Weave.

A more technical exposition of the various weaves may now follow : the plain weave naturally comes first. Let the reader bear in mind that all the black squares in the design and weave plans given in this weave and its variations show weft intersections in which the weft rides upon the top of the warp threads; and that the blank or white squares indicate that the warp in that position is uppermost, and the weft below. If the weft did not interlace with the warp in this manner all would be blanks and the formation of a woven fabric impossible.

Fig. 28 gives the design as already explained. This consists of two warp and two weft threads crossing each other at right angles. In coarse, open cloths, such as canvas, etc., two heald shafts would be sufficient. The draft or weave plan, which means the order in which the warp is drawn into the healds, would then be represented in A. The numbers on the right-hand side indicate the draft of the warp threads through the healds on the shafts in the order of their arrangement; and the figures at the bottom show the order of the weft picks. As explained before, where a great number of warp threads require to be dealt with, and concentration is necessary, as in fine cotton, worsted, and silk fabrics, four, six, or eight heald shafts are introduced in order to secure a better distribution of the warp threads, thus diminishing the crowding, reducing

FIG. 28.   A.   B.   C.   D.   E.   F.   G.

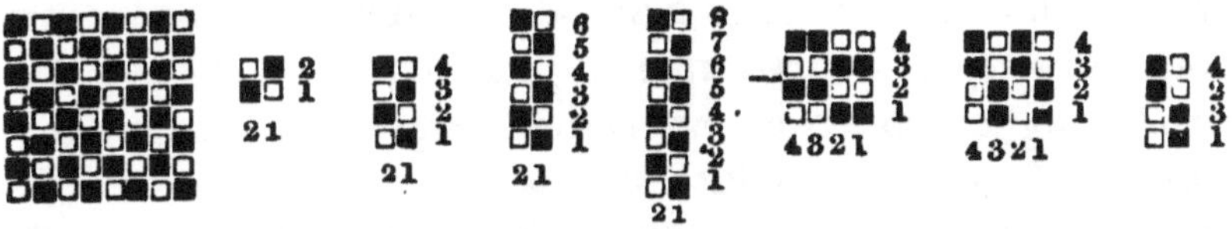

PLAIN CLOTH, WITH THE DESIGN, WEAVE PLANS, AND VARIATIONS.

the friction, and lessening the breakages of the threads that would otherwise occur in the weaving of closely compacted fabrics. In these cases the drafts B, C, and D would represent respectively the use of sets of healds of four, six, and eight shafts, and the order of warp drafts for them. In such drafts the shedding is easier as the threads pass each other with less friction, and both yarn and healds are opened more easily to take up broken threads when these occur.

Whilst two, four, six, or eight shafts are commonly used for plain cloth, any even number will give the same result, providing the warp threads are drafted in consecutive order, and the odd numbers of the shafts can be lifted together for one shed, and the even numbers together for the alternate one.

Some observations have already been made upon the

methods of ornamenting plain cloths, and a few more may be permitted, as it is quite a mistake to suppose that the plain weave is incapable of yielding ornamentation. It has been shown how tape stripes and checks, both in plain and coloured goods, can be produced. These will yield some very effective patterns for muslins and light zephyrs, whilst mock gauzes, in which a series of reed dents are left without warp threads, form another interesting class in plain weave fabrics, the beauty of which can be further enhanced by the introduction of coloured yarn.

The draft E shews a warp cord, and the draft F a weft cord or rep. The thickness of the cord in the warp may be carried to any extent by increasing the number of threads that form it, or it may be obtained by introducing a second warp of coarse yarn. The weft cord, or rep, by introducing catch cords at the selvages may have any number of picks put into one shed, and these can be bound down by one or more picks in the alternate shed. Of course in the power-loom this implies the introduction of an intermittent shedding arrangement. As in the warp cord so in the weft, coarse and fine counts may alternate to give the effect. By a combination of warp and weft cords squares of basket figures or checks can be produced in endless variety, which make not only useful but beautiful fabrics. A plain weave also forms a secure basis or ground for Jacquard figures.

In the interweaving of coarse and fine yarns of warp and weft it is necessary to exercise judgment and care in proportioning the quantities, and particularly in cord effects.

Calicoes and nearly all ordinary plain cloths are woven with what is technically called a skip-shaft draft. This is shown in the draft G, which has been explained before. The four heald shafts rise and fall as if they were two only as will be seen on a glance at the marginal figures.

WOVEN FABRICS.

The Three-Shaft Twill.

The three-shaft twill next comes under notice. This weave is known by many names, such as drill, regatta, Jean, Jeanette, Llama, etc. It is the first departure from the plain weave and is the simplest weave after it. It is worked, as its name indicates, by three shafts of healds which work independently of one another, rising and falling in regular sequence in the order of their arrangement from the front, 1, 2, 3, 1, 2, 3, in continuous repetitions. Its effect is to throw up distinct ridges of weft that run diagonally across the cloth, ascending from left to right. This is caused by the weft always passing under

FIG. 29.   FIG. 30.   FIG. 31.   FIG. 32.

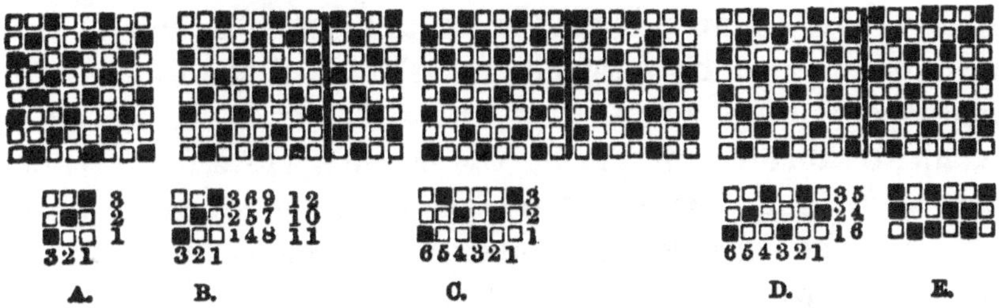

A.   B.   C.   D.   E.

THE 3-SHAFT TWILL, WITH DESIGNS, DRAFTS, ETC.

two warp threads and then over the next, as shown in the design (fig. 29) and its draft, A. It would appear from a casual glance at the design that it would not admit of much variation. It is, however, capable of considerable ornamentation, as is shown by the succeeding designs (figs. 30, 31, 32). Their respective drafts accompany them. In fig. 32 an alternative draft is given. A very bold twill figure, the diagonal rib, can be obtained by the employment of heavy yarns, and a fine effect by the use of fine yarns and closely set reeds. This twill is extensively used for light fancy lining cloths, and it generally forms a base for thicksets, velveteens, cords, and heavy fabrics. As a simple form of decoration, without colour, it is one of the most useful weaves in the whole list for diaper, herring-bone styles, and other goods. When employed in the woollen trade it is sometimes called the prunella twill, and it is known in the Bradford worsted trade as the Llama twill. By introducing coloured yarns and arranging them one and one, say black, blue, and white, the diagonal stripes may be crossed and form a series of checks or hair lines, giving a result that cannot be obtained from any other twill weave. In design, fig. 30, is shown an alternated reversal of the weave, forming what is called a herring-bone twill, from its supposed resemblance to the backbone of that fish. The next design (fig. 31) shows a transverse herring-bone; that is, the former design is made to have its line of direction across the cloth instead of, as before, along its length. Design fig. 32 is a diaper, its plan and draft being given in D. Weave plan E is that of a double twill, by which distinct colours can be obtained on each side of the fabric; for instance, with a white warp and a brown weft the warp would be thrown up, giving the fabric a white face, whilst the weft being thrown down would give a brown back. This may be regarded as a mock double cloth in which the backing is weft.

The examples given will show that this weave may be made a very useful one in the weaving-shed if a little judgment be exercised in its application and in the selection of suitable materials and colours. With these aids a great number of excellent effects may be obtained from this apparently comparatively inflexible weave.

In extensive designs of floral treatment, or other figures, this twill forms a good firm ground as a binder of either warp or weft threads.

In plain cloths it was stated that the yarns used in making them gave the best effects when the twine or twist was in the same direction, because yarns thus constructed imbed themselves better in each other, and so produce a more level and closely compacted cloth, which is the object sought. In twills, on the contrary, the development of the figure is a principal object sought, therefore the angle of direction of the twill should be in opposition, and not coincidence, to that of the yarns used in order to prevent the bedding effect of the alternate course, and so help to develop a clear and bold effect in the line of the twill.

The Four-Shaft Twill.

The next step brings before us the four-shaft twill. It must be borne in mind that every step forward made by the addition of another leaf of healds gives increasing capacity of figure production to the weaver, enabling the weaver, to borrow a metaphor from the church belfry, to ring an additional number of changes upon his instrument, the loom.

The four-shaft twill is variously known as the cassimere, kerseymere, serge, blanket, florentine, swansdown, crow, etc. It is in almost universal use in the weaving world, entering more or less into the composition of fabrics of every known textile fibre. It can be adapted to any counts of yarn and produce satisfactory results. In the fustian trade it is extensively used for plain-backed Genoa velvets, velverets, thickset cords, and an endless variety of patterns for suitings, trouserings, etc., in woollens, worsteds, fine hair lines, warp face figures, etc. It is impossible to enumerate in any reasonable space all the changes that can be made by the weave and draft of a four-shaft twill either alone or in combination with other weaves. The examples given herewith will, however, serve to point out to the student a portion of its capabilities, and indicate the lines upon which he may develop others for himself. The first design shown (fig. 33) is the ordinary disposition of this twill as seen in its common use. It is accompanied by its weave plan and draft, A, as usual. In the next (fig. 34) is shown the herring-bone or ticking

COTTON WEAVING.

stripe, a design much used in making bed-ticking and pillow-case fabrics. The draft is shown at B, the weave being the same as A.

The next design (fig. 35) shows a check formation which may be extended to any size by repeated drafts and

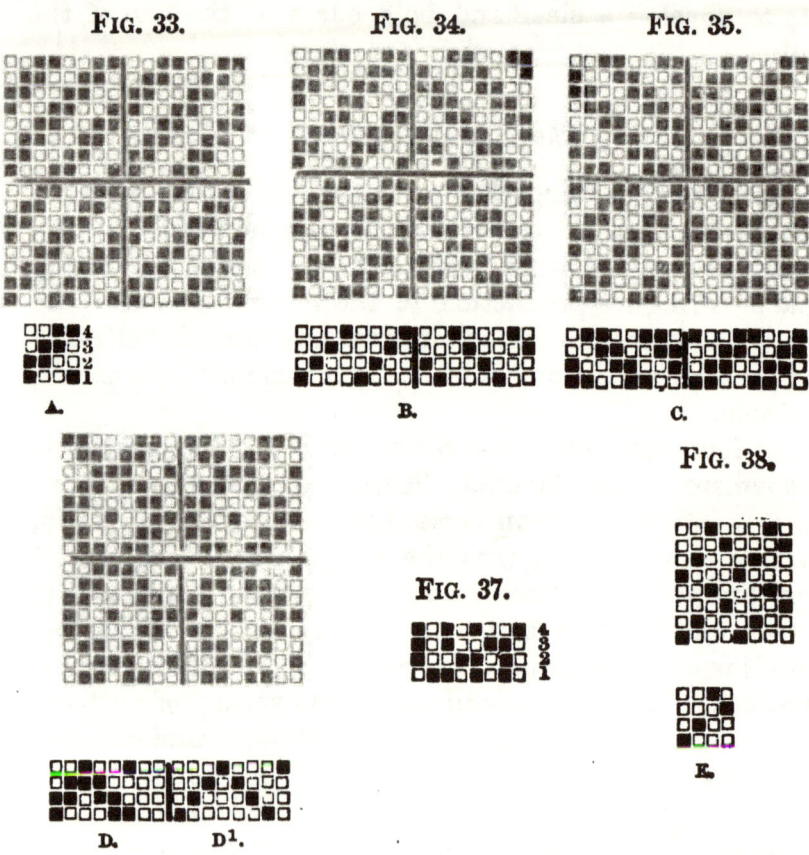

THE 4-SHAFT TWILL: DESIGNS, WEAVE PLANS, AND DRAFTS.

threads. The weave plan appears in C, whilst the draft is a repeat of B, fig. 34. Many beautiful effects can be produced by this weave and method of drafting.

The following design (fig. 36) is one for a diaper cloth, and its weave plan and draft are shown in D and D'.

The next design (fig. 37) is that of a double twill. In

this the face may be made very fine, and the back be weighted with much coarser material. It is mostly used in cotton quiltings and mixed goods of cotton warp and woollen wefts. The amount of material put into the fabric will, to a certain extent, govern the application of the rule previously laid down regarding the direction of the twist of the yarns used. Where the warp is used in the production of the face cloth, the same regard to the direction of the twist is not imperative; it is when the warp and weft are equally balanced in counts that the observance of the rule becomes important.

In design fig. 38 the satin twill is delineated with its accompanying weave E. This form of twill though not perfect, is used for the bulk of cloths having the greatest portion of either their warp or weft brought to the surface.

The Five-Shaft Twill.

The five-shaft twill is the next on the roll. This is used for heavy fabrics, such as drills, sateens, doeskins, damasks, etc. In fancy diaper cloths it affords great scope for the production of varieties. It is the first perfect satin twill, and it yields many derivatives. Satin twills give a peculiar angle when formed by warp threads. They yield greater strength in the lengthway of the fabric than most other weaves of this type. The reader must here be guarded against the possible confusion that may arise between the terms satin and sateen. The former is the weave employed in making the silk fabric termed satin, in which the weave effect is obtained by throwing the warp to the surface, thus showing the threads running parallel with the length of the fabric; in the sateen weave the weft is thrown to the surface, and the line of the visible threads upon it runs across the cloth from side to side. When the sateen or weft twill is used, the satin or warp twill is simply thrown to the back of the fabric, and *vice*

COTTON WEAVING.

versâ. This principle governs both of these weaves whenever they are employed.

In the design fig. 39 is given the ordinary weave of the five-shaft twill; A shows its weave plan and draft.

In design fig. 40 the satin weave is given, and in B its plan and draft.

In design fig. 41 a fancy twill is given, and in C its weave is shown. As will be seen by referring to A (fig. 39) there is merely an additional black square introduced and placed below each of those in the original plan. This

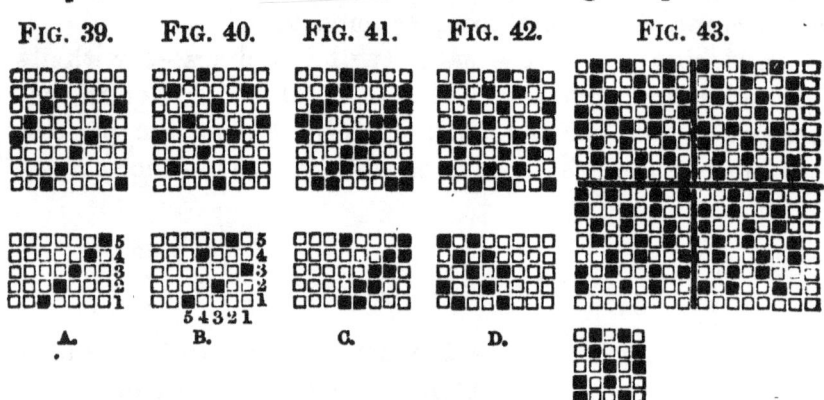

THE 5-SHAFT TWILL DESIGN, ETC.

makes two each in the run where there was only one before. An excellent effect is obtained from it.

The design shown in fig. 42 will give a very firm weave, in which there will be no risk of the threads of the fabric slipping. It is very suitable for linings. Its plan appears in D.

Design fig. 43 is derived from that shown in fig. 40, and is obtained by the introduction of another dot for each of those in the former design. Its plan is shown at E.

All the drafts in these examples are straight-over drafts. Numerous other weaves might be brought forward to show the wide range of usefulness of this twill, but those given are their foundations and the ones from which they are derived. The combinations that can be made of these yield many interesting results, and the exercise of developing them would be most useful to the student.

As a ground for figured effects the five-shaft twill is much used by designers for all kinds of silk, cotton, linen, woollen and worsted goods.

The Six-Shaft Twill.

This is deservedly a favourite basis for almost every class of fabric, and with colours in warp and weft will give numerous combinations.

In design fig. 44 is given the basic arrangement of the weave, showing equal flushing of warp and weft. The weave plan, A, it will be seen from the figures on the margin, is a straight-over draft.

Design fig. 45 is also a form of twill very frequently seen; in this there are more warp threads brought to the surface. The weave plan, B, shows it to be a straight draft.

The next design (fig. 46) divides the diagonal figure into two portions, bringing a warp thread up between the floating weft threads. In this design, instead of floating three and sinking three, they float two, sink one and float one. This arrangement increases the firmness of the fabric from that of fig. 44, but sacrifices some capacity for a display of colours. The weave plan is C, a straight draft.

In design fig. 47 is given a variation, suitable and in use for diaper patterns. In the weave plan, D, the draft is shown by the figures at the margin.

Design fig. 48 exhibits a satin as made on six shafts. The weave, E, shows it a straight draft. This is termed one of the imperfect satins, though largely used as a ground for figured effects.

There are numerous derivatives from all regular twills,

COTTON WEAVING.

producing the effect of several portions of a twill combined in one weave. The six-shaft twill under notice affords numerous examples, one of which, with the explanation of its formation will suffice to show how others can be con-

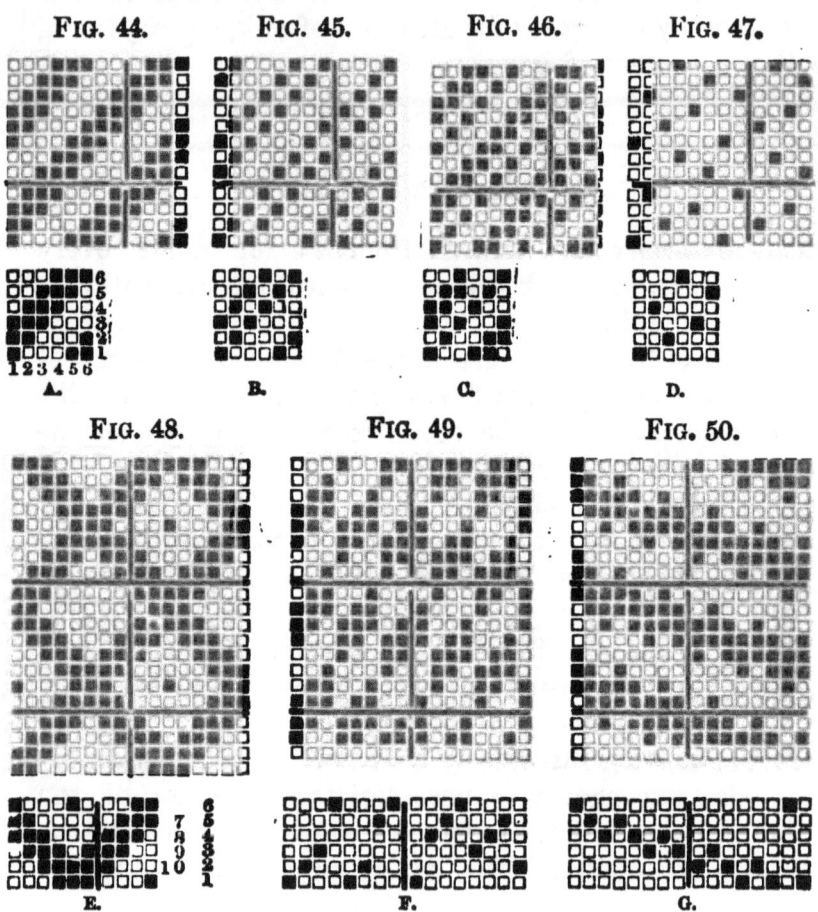

THE 6-SHAFT TWILL: DESIGNS, WEAVE PLANS, AND DRAFTS.

structed. For this weave plan A (fig. 44) may be taken as a foundation. The number for counting off determines the number of threads to be used in each part before changing. The number to be left out shows the number of threads to be skipped, and also gives the number of the thread on which the next change will take place.

As an illustration, design fig. 49 is given. The number of threads used in this are three for each change, whilst two threads are left for each skip. By referring to the figures given at the bottom of the weave plan, A (fig. 44), the arrangement of the threads in the design can be easily followed by observing this rule. The full repeat is shown, F being the draft.

Design fig. 50 is another form of construction, G being the weave plan. In these drafts the warp threads are evenly distributed over the shafts, no shaft being overloaded. From a weaver's point of view, this is a great advantage in weaving many fabrics composed of fine, tender yarns. The number of threads used for a change may be increased, as, for instance, a design may be constructed from the weave plan, A (fig. 44), by counting six and skipping two. In fact, the capability of changing is almost inexhaustible, and offers a fine field for study to the textile student. In every twill, whatever may be the number of shafts, this system can be utilized with the most satisfactory results. These remarks will obviate the necessity of going over the same ground again in other examples to be brought forward. They will also be found sufficient to convey the necessary practical information for developing new ideas and obtaining fresh and useful weaves.

The Seven-Shaft Twill.

The seven-shaft twill, which we now proceed to notice, conducts the student another step forward in the path in which he obtains increased capacity. The first design given (fig. 51) is a satin, A being the weave plan. This is a perfect satin, as we may observe, in passing, are all satins that are formed by an odd number of threads in the straight-over draft, or in the number required to form a complete pattern. There are many rules given for the placing of the wefts dots or intersections in a satin weave, but the simplest method is the best. This is to take the first number after one that is not a measure of the shafts or repeat threads. Thus three would be the first number in seven after one, therefore this may be used to count with as follows:

$$1, 6, 4, 2, 7, 5, 3.$$

The dots represent the seven shafts or threads. This gives one plan of intersections by the use of three as a measure. But four may be used also as it is not a

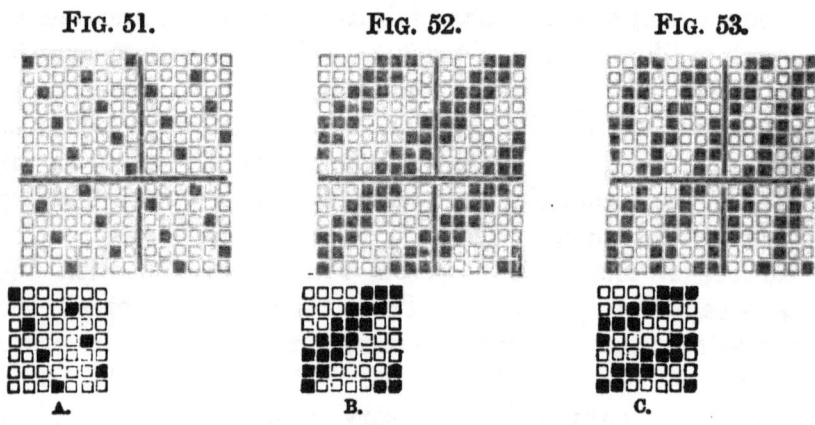

FIG. 51. FIG. 52. FIG. 53.

A. B. C.

THE 7-SHAFT TWILL: DESIGNS AND WEAVE PLANS.

multiple of seven, and this would give the following arrangement:

$$1, 3, 5, 7, 2, 4, 6.$$

Upon this principle the intersecting dots of any satin may be found; and on reference to design fig. 51 it will be seen how these latter figures have been practically applied.

Design fig. 52 is a regular seven-shaft twill, with its accompanying weave plan, B, a straight draft.

Design fig. 53 is a derivative twill with a more vertical

figure, obtained from the satin arrangement of fig. 51. Its weave plan is given in c.

The remarks made about the six-shaft twill apply with equal force to this and all other twills, so that there is no need to increase the number of examples, as, by following the instructions given, any number can be constructed with facility, whilst by combinations with other twills, reverse drafts, and colours, the capacity for obtaining variation of effect will be found to have hardly any limit.

The Eight-Shaft Twill.

The eight-shaft twill is again richer in its effects and variations than the preceding. In design fig. 54 is given the ordinary eight-shaft twill, straight draft and weave plan, A.

Design fig. 55 is a fancy broken twill, formed from the weave plan, A, fig. 54. The draft is given in B, and the extended weave plan in c. This example will prove a good study for the student, because a further fresh disposition of the draft would bring out another formation equally useful and ornamental.

Design fig. 56 is a diaper arrangement constructed from the V draft D, its weave plan being given in E. It will now be quite obvious that any other eight-shaft weave with the same draft would give further novelties.

Design fig. 57 is a satin with its weave, F, the draft being straight over.

Design fig. 58 is a combination on eight shafts of design fig. 54 and its satin arrangement, which will give a stripe effect. Naturally it will be evident that the width of the stripe can be increased by an extension of the draft given at G. The weave plan is the same as A of design fig. 54.

It would be quite impossible to give any adequate conception of the number of changes that can be brought out

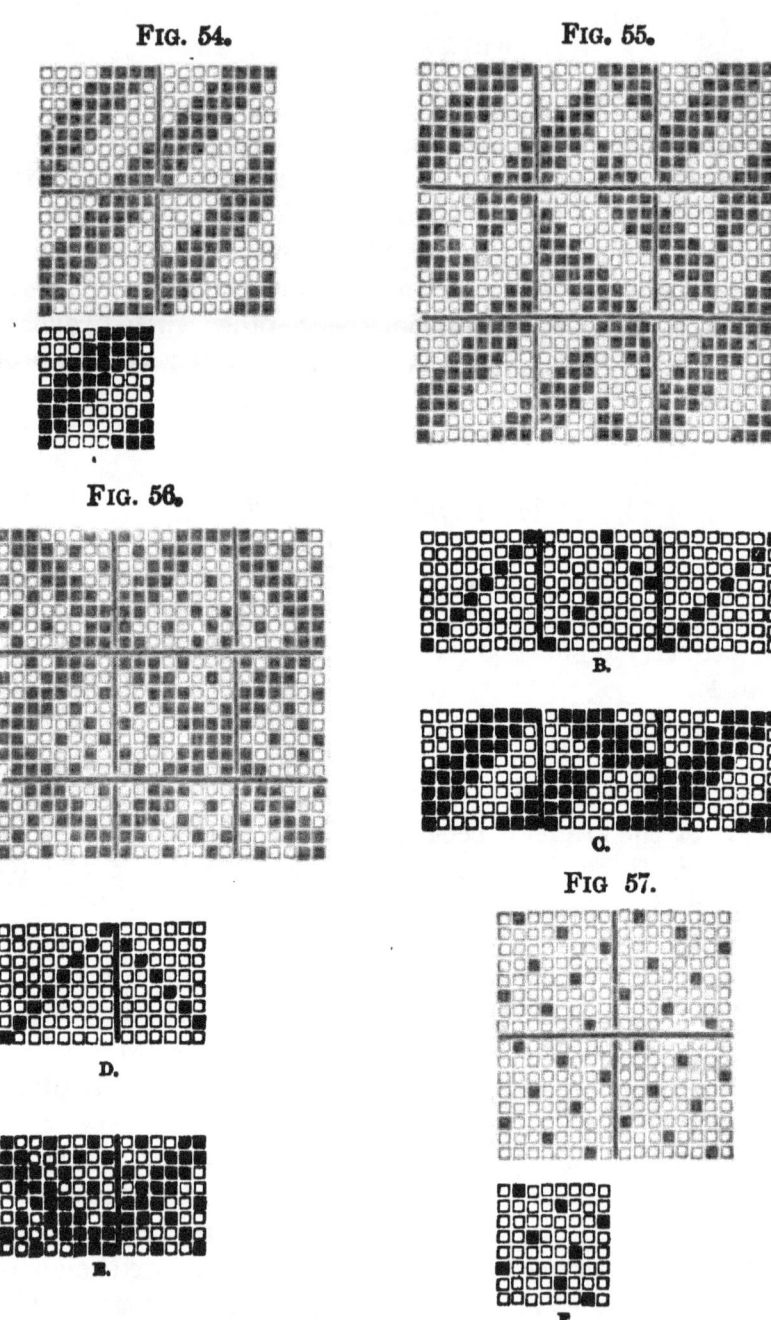

THE 8-SHAFT TWILL AND VARIATIONS.

from the drafts, etc., but the examples given will serve to represent the main features. As foundation weaves they will produce highly desirable results when wrought in well-chosen materials.

FIG. 58.

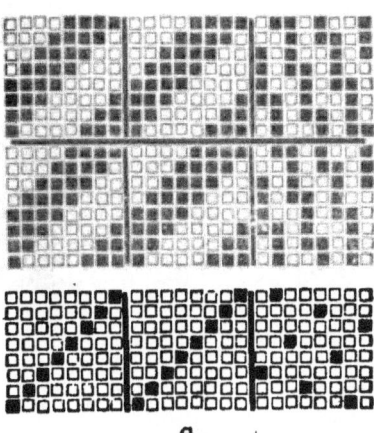

G.

THE 8-SHAFT TWILL (continued).

The Nine-Shaft Twill.

The first design given here (fig. 59), is for a satin twill, the weave plan being given in A; straight draft.

Design fig. 60 is one of the many forms used for fancy weaves in either stripes, checks, or colours. Its weave plan, B; straight draft.

Design fig. 61 is a broken form of the twill, giving novel effects. The draft is shown at C. This, to the technical student, is an instructive and suggestive design, as though, in reality, there are only nine threads, yet by the use of the weave plan, D, their skilful distribution gives in the design shown twenty-seven threads to the round or full figure. This figure may be re-arranged by the alteration of the draft. Care, however, requires to be taken to compose the draft in such a manner that, as

FIG. 59.   FIG. 60.

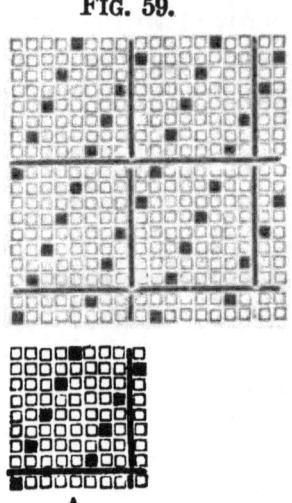
A.

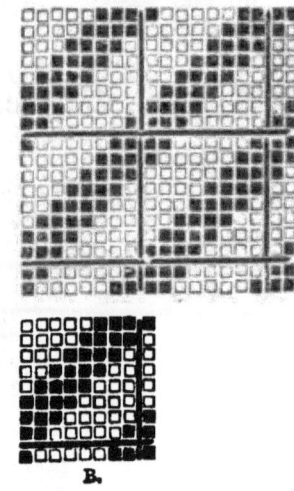
B.

FIG. 61.

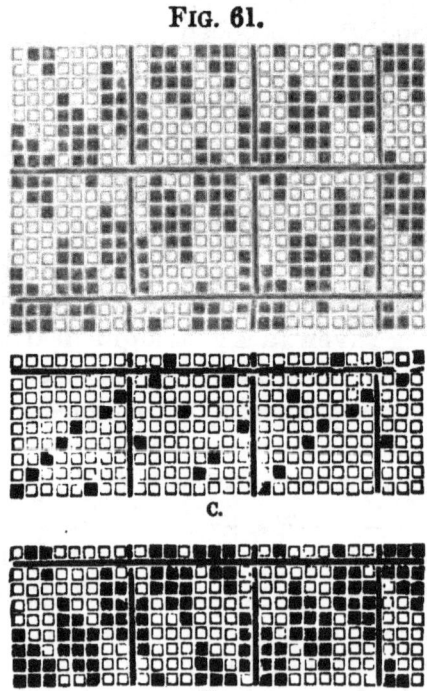
C.

D.

THE 9-SHAFT TWILL, ETC.

in D, the shafts shall carry an equal number of threads, namely, $9 \times 3 = 27$. This gives three repeats of the nine threads to one figure of the fancy pattern. This required care observed, a perfect joining of the pattern will be made.

From designs such as are here given any number of patterns can be obtained by a slight study of the draft and weave arrangements, the essential point for consideration being to make them neat, chaste, and beautiful, so that when wrought into suitable kinds of fabrics, they may prove of high commercial value.

The Ten-Shaft Twill.

This is the last of this series proposed to be given, as it may be fairly assumed that their fundamental principles will then have been fully treated.

The first design (fig. 62) is a ten-shaft satin, with its weave plan, A; straight draft. If sateens are required to be made on any number of shafts, all that is necessary is to bring the back of the satin cloth to the face; that is, to work one shaft up successively all through the series, and the others down.

In design fig. 63, which is for a fancy fabric, the figure is of the diagonal type, having combined with it a Vandyke border; B is the weave plan; straight draft.

From fig. 63 is derived the next design (fig. 64) with the B weave plan, and the same straight draft. In this way it yields a broken-up effect, very useful in woollen and kindred fabrics, or where type effects of a similar character are required.

In the next design (fig. 65) an extension is made in order to show the joinings of the figures; C is the draft, and D the weave plan. By doubling or tripling this form of draft, a very complicated series of figures could be obtained that would appear as if woven with a Jacquard machine.

FIG. 62.　　　　　　　　FIG. 63.

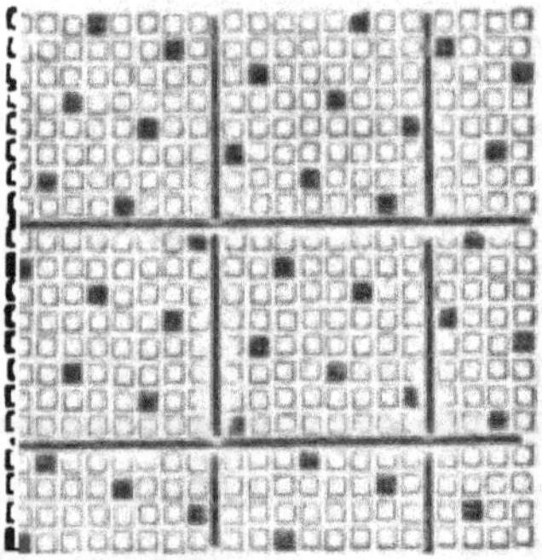

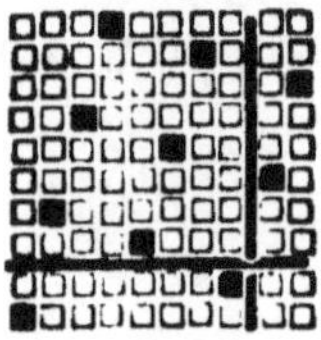

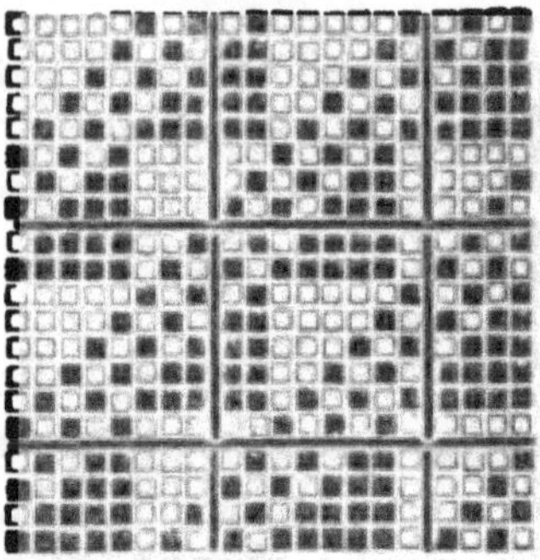

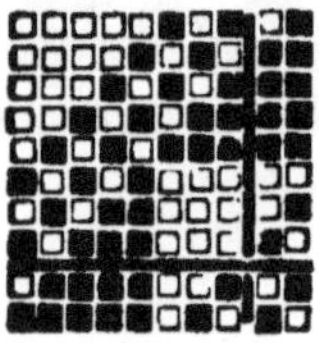

A.　　　　　　　　　　B.

FIG. 64.　　　　　　　　FIG. 65.

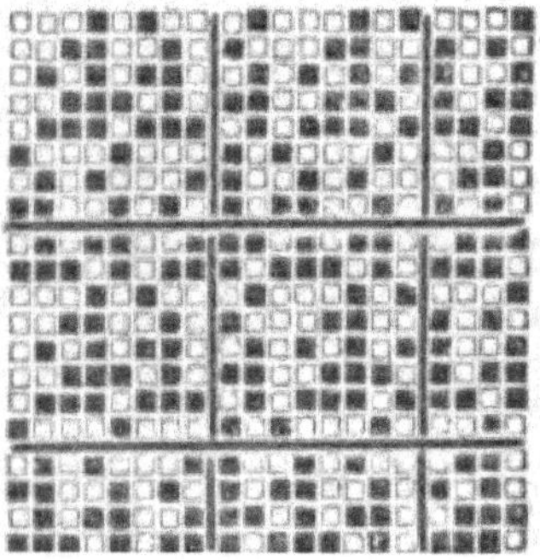

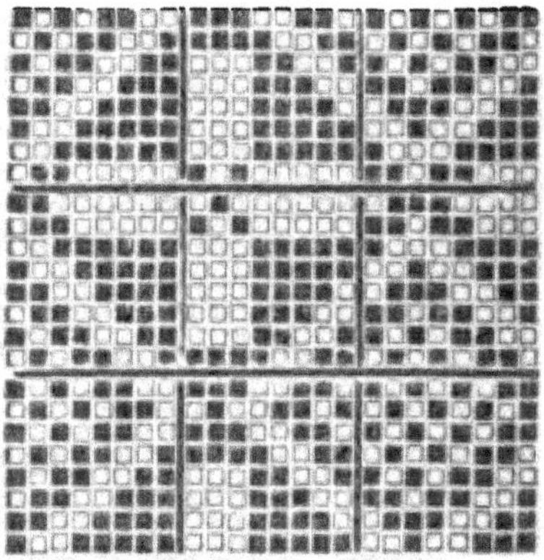

C.

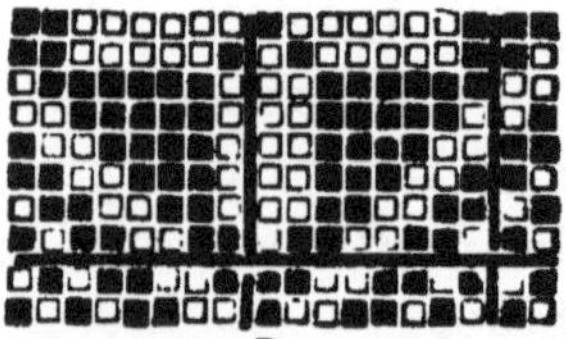

D.

THE 10-SHAFT TWILL, ETC.

The exigencies of space preclude any further exposition of this phase of the subject. That already given constitutes a sufficient guide for the development and treatment of all designs capable of being made upon any shedding mechanism or apparatus in use, with the exception of the Jacquard machine, which requires a special description. The changes capable of being developed and wrought by the adaptations and combinations of the weaves and drafts already given are almost infinite, and if executed with knowledge, skill, and taste will prove of considerable monetary value.

In larger designs, such as damask figures, the satin weaves act as binders; or the ground may be warp satin, and the figures weft or sateen twills. In these classes of goods two colours are generally used, unless they are fabrics intended for bleaching. One colour is used for the warp, and another for the weft. The ground is preferentially obtained by a weft effect, as the figures stand out more boldly when constructed of a warp satin. Hence all the threads composing the figure effects will have the twill running lengthwise of the cloth, whilst the ground twill, composed of the weft, will run across.

Throughout the preceding remarks, it has been endeavoured to expound the principles of the various weaves and their combinations from a practical standpoint, in order that no difficulty might be encountered by the student in at once making a practical application of them.

Double and Multiple Cloth Weaving.

The student of the textile arts who is only familiar with the plain calico weaving which is so extensive in the cotton, will learn, perhaps with surprise, that double cloths are commonly made in some districts, and that triple cloths are occasionally made, whilst manifold cloths can be made in very ordinary looms with some little extra adjuncts. In order that the student may in some degree be equipped for and prepared to meet all requirements that may be made upon him, some description of these modes of procedure may now be given.

A true double cloth is really two cloths woven at one operation in the same loom. They may, when removed from the loom, be perfectly separate, or combined at one or both sides, or may adhere to one another more or less closely by connecting threads, or be so closely interwoven with each other in that manner that only persons with some technical knowledge really could know the true nature of the fabric. The two cloths may differ in pattern, in fineness of material, and even be of materials quite different from one another in their origin, mode of construction, and the weave by which they are put together. Two, three, or even more pieces of cloth of the width of the loom might be woven together, and being united at the sides when taken from the loom would open out into one wide sheet, three or four times the width of the loom in which it had been produced. Or two widths might be made together and joined at each side, when the fabric would be a cylindrical tube if opened out. In weaving this it might be interwoven at given distances as required, and being cut across at these, the cut lengths would form seamless bags. Many millions of these, popularly called "mutton bags," are made in Lancashire for the Australian and New Zealand frozen meat trade, each bag being of sufficient dimensions to receive the carcase of a sheep.

When double cloths are made reversible they have either two warp or weft faces. When extra weight is required, as in most woollen fabrics, and in some cotton ones, as quiltings, a backing of coarser material, either in the warp or weft, may be attached to the face cloth by what are termed stitching threads, which may be more or less in number, according to the degree of attachment required. In many cases fabrics are thus made three and even fourfold, not only for obtaining a fine face, strength, warmth, or weight at a low cost, but for getting strange effects and fancy figures by making the cloths interchangeable. Of course when double cloths are produced the maker is endeavouring to meet some distinct requirement, and it is in this way that tubular fabrics, hose pipes and sacks have been produced.

The fundamental principles of these peculiar weaves are simply and clearly stated, and may be easily understood by an examination of the following weaves, in which the dots represent that the heald shaft, and consequently the warp thread is uppermost. The figures at the foot of the weaves show the picks of weft, and those at the side the order of drawing-in the warp threads on the heald shafts. With a warp in two colours, and a pattern two white and two blue threads, the white portion of the warp would be on the first and second shafts, and the blue on the third and fourth shafts. If this pattern was woven with one shuttle, and with the skip-shaft draft of the plain weave given at the opening of these weave expositions, in which the first and third threads would be taken for the first shed, and the second and fourth for the alternate shed, only a single cloth would be formed having a stripe pattern. But by the use of two shuttles, one containing white and the other blue weft, with the weave shown in fig. 66, two separate cloths would be obtained, one all white and the other all blue. The explanation of this is as follows :—On the first pick with the blue shuttle a shed is formed for its passage by the whole of the white warp being lifted above the shuttle-race, and one-half of the blue warp as well. The blue pick taken through the shed by the shuttle gives one-half of the blue cloth ; on the return passage of the blue shuttle in the next shed the blue cloth is completed, without mixture with the white warp, because the whole of the white warp is still kept up, whilst the second half of the blue warp has been lifted, and the first half sent down, as will be seen by the blank square on the second pick of the figure. In the next movement the white shuttle comes into work. The third pick is now made, all the blue and one-half of the white warp being sunk, whilst the shuttle makes its passage, the other half of the white warp being kept up to form the shed. This pick of the white weft gives one-half of the white fabric, and when the white sheds have changed their positions, and the return pick of the white shuttle is made, the white fabric will be completed, and two separate cloths, one blue and one white, will have been formed.

If one shuttle only had been used with the above weave the cloths would have been united at the selvages, and a tubular fabric would have been made. It is in this manner hose-pipe, lamp-wick, tucks, bags, etc., are formed. By the addition of a second set of four-heald shafts, making eight shafts in all, and having each coloured warp upon one distinct set, squares for vestings, fancy dress goods, bed-spreads, etc., can easily be developed. All that is necessary is to enlarge upon the weave (fig. 66) just given. Though in the last illustration two shafts were allotted to the blue warp and two to the white warp, there is no reason why ten shafts, or any other number, should not be used for one warp and an equal number for the other, or three, four, or six sets might be used for as many coloured warps and wefts. The principle would be the same, and these are merely adduced to partially show its capacity of application. The different sizes of squares depend upon the number of repeats of each colour over its own set of shafts, and the corresponding number of treads of the warp and passage of the same coloured shuttle until the square is completed. This done, another set of shafts having another coloured warp with its corresponding coloured shuttle is brought into operation.

The weave given in fig. 67 is one for two colours, blue and white, or any other two, warped end and end and drawn in as shown by the marginal figures; the draft on

WOVEN FABRICS.

each set of shafts being repeated to the extent necessary to get the required dimensions, and the treads of each section picked over for a corresponding number of times of blue and white shuttles, alternate squares of blue and white double cloth will be formed.

Fig. 68 gives a double twill cloth, the weft twill being

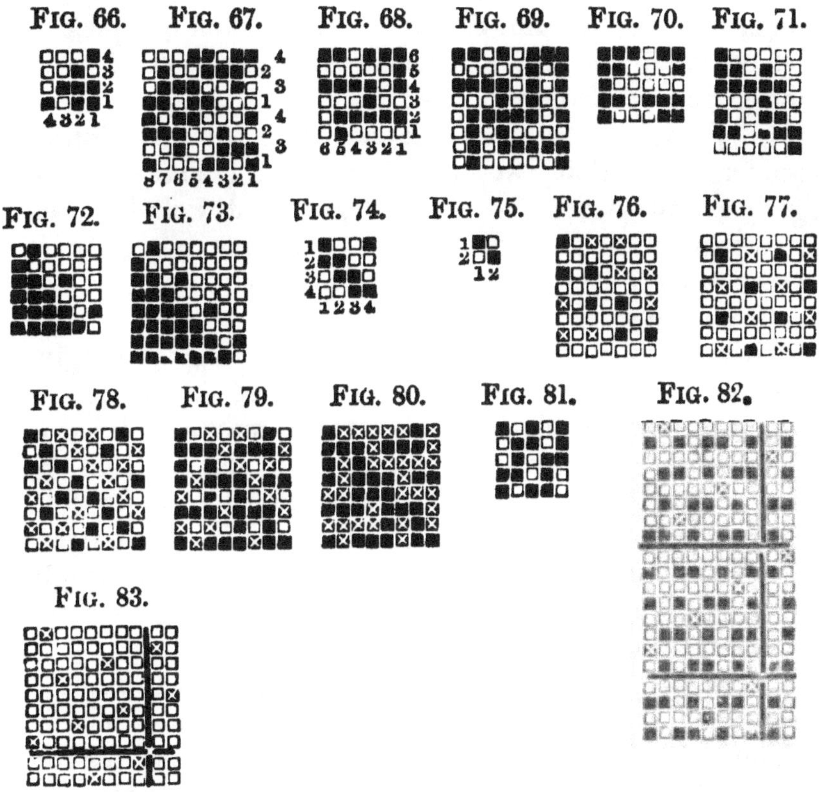

FIG. 66. FIG. 67. FIG. 68. FIG. 69. FIG. 70. FIG. 71.

FIG. 72. FIG. 73. FIG. 74. FIG. 75. FIG. 76. FIG. 77.

FIG. 78. FIG. 79. FIG. 80. FIG. 81. FIG. 82.

FIG. 83.

DOUBLE CLOTHS: WEAVES, ETC.

inside the cylinder cloth that it forms. The figures on the margin show the draft, and those at the bottom the threads. This is the three-shaft twill.

The next design (fig. 69) is the four-shaft twill double cloth. The weave given in fig. 68 is also used for this when employed for bags and tubular fabrics.

The next (fig. 70) is a weave that will produce three

cloths in a loom of, say, thirty inches wide, that when woven and opened out will be ninety inches wide, or three times the width of the loom. We commend it to the attention of young students.

If the next weave (fig. 71) had a warp of three colours, warped thread and thread of each in alternation, say brown, blue, and cream, the weft to be picked one pick of each colour in succession, then three fabrics each of a distinct colour would be produced.

Fig. 72 is the same as the last with the variation of requiring only that two threads of each colour shall go together and two picks of each coloured weft be used to correspond. This does away with the necessity of using the pick-and-pick loom as three boxes on one side would do the work.

The next (fig. 73) worked on this principle will give four pieces of plain cloth, each two shafts producing a separate piece of cloth. This system may be carried to any extent, but its principal value lies in the fact that, by the introduction of a stitching thread, the whole four fabrics may be made of any thickness and be bound into one solid cloth. Such cloths if made in woollen might be felted, and of course would contain three or four times the quantity of material as the case might be.

To attempt the exposition of the principles in the fullest detail, and to give minute particulars of the constructions of double cloth fabrics, would require a volume for the task, and which, it will be obvious, cannot be given. A few examples of the system adopted in ordinary practice for backing cloths must suffice.

For backing a twill face such as is given in fig. 74, a suitable backing would be that shown in fig. 75. The first step is the face (fig. 76), and fig. 77 shows the back; fig. 78 gives face and back cloths combined; fig. 79 shows the face warp up to admit the back pick, and fig. 80 the back warp down to admit the face pick.

In these several figures a complete analysis of the

method of backing a cloth is given, and it illustrates the principle upon which all such fabrics with a twill face are constructed. The crosses in the design show the position of the stitching or back points all through. A close study of these figures will thoroughly reveal the operation. The point to be determined is whether the stitch is to be obtained from a plain or satin weave. The method of obtaining the intersecting points of any satin weave has already been given, and the rule can be applied to double cloths. But the face weave, of whatever kind it may be, must always govern the back weave, because the face weave may have to be repeated in such a manner as to make it a measure for the back weave. If the flushing of the weft is somewhat long, the stitching must be got as near to the centre of the float, or flush, as possible, and with the face pick going immediately before and immediately following it. To illustrate these remarks fig. 81 is given, which is a five-shaft twill; and fig. 82 shows the repeat, so that it may be stitched with a ten-shaft satin plan. An examination of the two figures will show that the stitching is equally distributed, the face pick preceding and following the stitcher. The principle of the matter is in the count which the backing or satin weave must give. In figs. 82 and 83 it will be seen that two is the count, beginning from the left-hand side, and this counting follows the angle of the twill.

The best practice in laying out for fancy double cloths is to design the face twill or figure separately, and should it require a warp back the vertical spaces in the design are left vacant if the backing is one of face and one of back threads; if two face threads to one of back, then the design would be for the face weave two vertical rows dotted, and one row blank, and so on in this order through the design. If a weft back is required, then the transverse rows are left vacant according to the disposition of the weft picks. After duly considering a face cloth design, a suitable backing weave is drawn out on separate design paper.

This gives a complete idea of the upper and lower surfaces of the cloth, and the backing weave is then run in on the vacant spaces left in the face design. It may, and does often, occur that many designs are so peculiar that it is difficult to devise a proper backing weave for them. In these cases an irregular satin twill will often be found useful. It is of no moment how irregular the stitches may be if they do not show on the face cloth. Judgment must, of course, be exercised to prevent such blemishes. If the illustrations herewith given are carefully studied, they will be found to afford a sufficient exposition of the principles involved in the construction of double cloths, and the practice of them will make an expert.

Crimped Cloths.

In fancy woven goods a crimped effect can often be introduced with great advantage to embellish the fabric. It contrasts very effectively with any other weave with which it may be combined, and gives ornamental results that cannot otherwise be obtained. At the time of writing this (1893), and for some while past, it has been highly popular as a component part of fancy woven fabrics.

In order to get the best effects, it is necessary to carefully consider the various combinations forming the fabric. A certain relationship that is unchanging, and that gives the maximum of beautiful effect, always exists between the different weaves when used in combination, and it is for the textile artist to discover and employ this in preference to the other dispositions not so good. The chief point to be regarded is the careful handling of the plain weave upon which the crimped effect is to be placed. The portion of the warp to be devoted to crimping, must be run upon a separate beam, for the reception of which provision must be made in the loom. This beam, which we may term the crimp beam, must be very lightly weighted compared with the other, in order to permit the slay, when beating up the weft pick, to draw the warp from the crimp beam into horizontal ridges, as it is woven. The warp upon the other beam must be kept in a state of tight or high tension, as this is required, and also gives a better contrasting effect.

Fig. 84 shows a combination weave of satin, plain, and cord. As far as designing any weave is concerned, it is comparatively simple. Ribs of different widths may be constructed, and various arrangements of colours adopted at will. The greater the number of weft picks put in, the

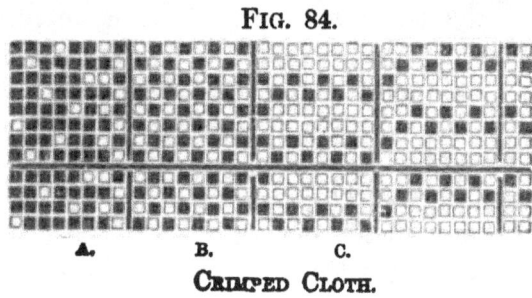

FIG. 84.

A.   B.   C.

CRIMPED CLOTH.

better will be the result. Fancy twills, or figure developments, may take the place of plain stripes.

In fig. 84, A shows a six-shaft satin stripe face effect; B the plain or crimped stripe; and C the corded stripe. Any number of ends may be drawn on each set of shafts, but it is advisable not to unduly extend the width of the various stripes, but to keep them in a proper proportion to each other.

The principle of the construction of these cloths is here pointed out, and all that is required further for the production of very saleable and popular fabrics is taste and judgment.

Cords, Velvets, Velveteens, Plushes, Moleskins, etc.

The term velvet, though properly belonging to a silken fabric, is now also generally applied to fine cotton fabrics made in imitation thereof. The pile of silk velvet is made from the warp, that of all cotton imitations from the weft. To be correctly described, the latter should be termed cotton velvets, to distinguish them from the heavier makes of the same class of cloths which are usually termed velveteens. Silk velvets are always made by the insertion of wires into the shed of the warp, either by the hand of the weaver or by automatic mechanism. In many cases these wires are formed into a knife-blade at one end, so that as they are withdrawn from the other they cut the pile; in other cases the plain wire is used, and the pile cut afterwards. Worsted velvets and plushes are formed in the same manner. Cotton velvets, velveteens, and other cotton-pile fabrics, are made differently, the pile always being formed by the weft, and for this the wire is not applicable. After these goods are woven the pieces are subjected to another process, that of pile-cutting, in which, either by hand or machine, the pile is cut in a direction parallel with the length of the fabric, in this respect also differing from the silk fabric, where the cutting is in the direction of its width. Dressing, dyeing, finishing, and making-up complete the goods for the market.

In the classes of cotton fabrics named above there are numerous varieties, but the examples given below are selected from the best in general use to-day, and will serve the requirements of illustration at present, which is simply to show their principles of construction, and that they belong to the division of double cloths.

Our first illustration (fig. 85) is of a tabby or plain-backed velvet; it is made on six shafts, with a straight draft, and eight picks to the round.

Our next (fig. 86) is a weave variation for velveteen, made on six shafts, and with nine picks to the round.

The third (fig. 87) is also a velveteen made on six shafts, with twelve picks to the round.

Fig. 88 represents a very popular class of velveteens, made on six shafts, with twelve picks to the round, con-

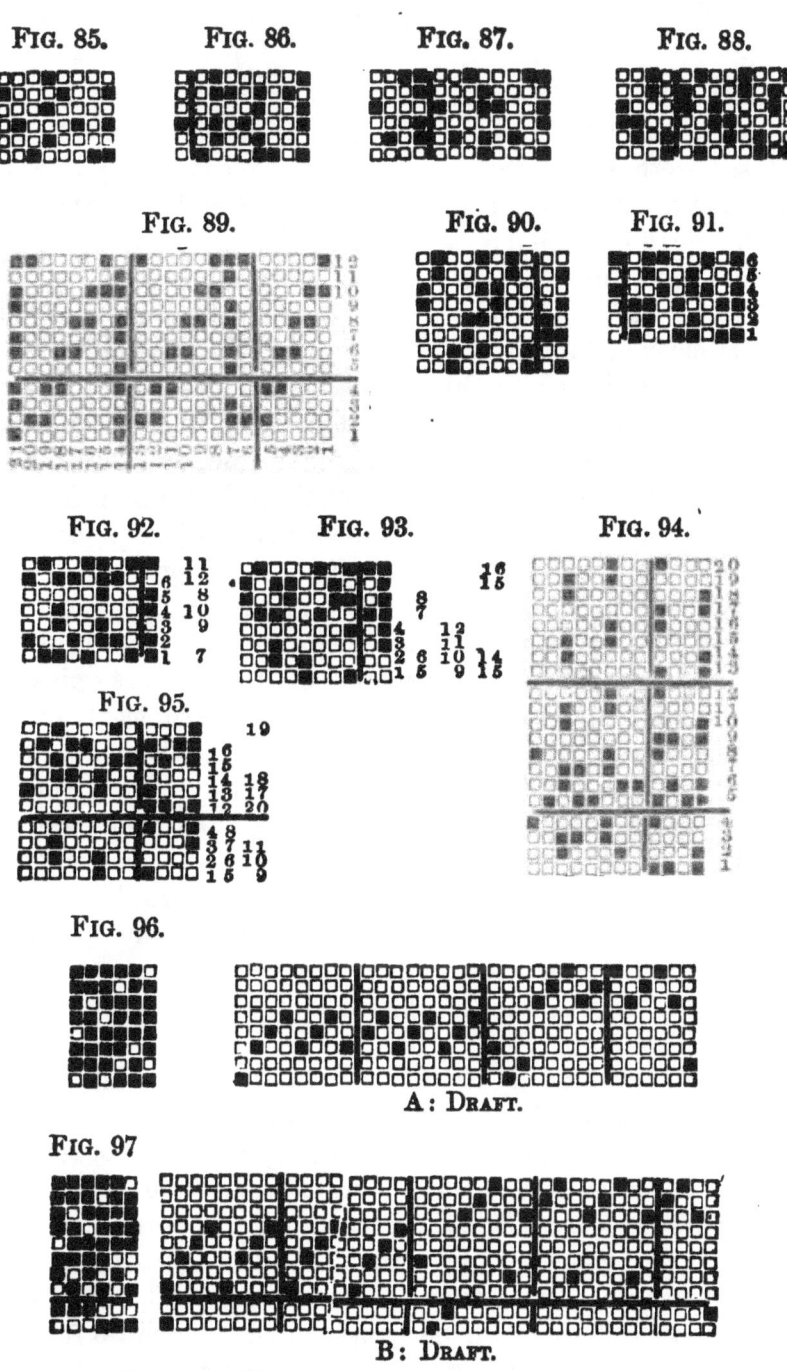

VELVETS, VELVETEENS, CORDS, AND PLUSHES.

taining 1,860 threads in 30 inches of width, equal to 62 warp threads in 1 inch. The warp yarn is 16^s or 18^s, the weft counts and number of picks according to requirement, this being generally a given weight per yard.

The next (fig. 89) is a velvet with a jean back. The weave shows how the pile and the stitching threads are put in, which will convey a good idea of the construction of this class of fabrics. The twelve shafts on which it is made are numbered on the margin of the plan; the treads or weft picks at the bottom from 1 to 21. The pile or weft face is formed by six picks and the stitching thread, binder, or back, as it is indifferently termed, is the seventh tread or pick; then follows another six picks for pile, which brings us to the fourteenth, forming the second stitching or binder pick tying the face and back together; and, lastly follows six more pile picks and one more stitching pick, completing the round of twenty-one picks. Thus, it will be seen, eighteen pile picks are used, with three jean twill picks for binder and back, which gives a proper and proportionate construction. The ordinary four-shaft kerseymere twill could be used for the back, but if six picks of pile weft were put between each pick of the twill back, twenty-eight picks to the round would be required, as in all backed cloths; whatever may be the weaves used for the back and face they must work in harmony with each other throughout the round, or the result will be imperfect.

Fig. 90 exhibits a ribbed velveteen, made on eight shafts, straight draft and ten picks to the round. This requires good yarns, uniformly cylindrical, to make a neat fabric, because the rib is formed from them.

Coming to the cords, which constitute another class of heavy cotton goods, kindred to the latter, the first specimen is given in the design of a thickset-cord (fig. 91), the least in size that can be constructed. The pile forms two separate cords, and in the cutting process the cutter runs his knife between the threads Nos. 2 and 5 (see the numbers on the margin of the design, fig. 91). In the construction of the fabric a tube or longitudinal cell is formed to admit of the cutting process, and to separate the pile into the lines which form the peculiar feature of cords. The back of this example is constructed in the same manner as a velveteen, being composed of two single jean twills. The best reed in which to make it would be a 36ˢ Stockport count, and a 14ˢ single warp, with sufficient weft picks to give a weight of 10 ozs. per yard.

Fig. 92 is a seven-shaft cord, the draft of which is given in figures on the margin.

Fig. 93 is a double jean round top cord, eight shafts, sixteen ends draft, and ten picks to the round.

Fig. 94 is the analysis of a cable cord on twenty warp threads.

Fig. 95 is the reduction to ten shafts, draft on the margin; twelve picks to the round.

Fig. 96, with the draft A, will produce the hunter's cord. It is made on eight shafts, with a thirty end draft, which is given in A, and six picks to the round. With this design and draft fancy cords with stripes of various colours can be made with the greatest facility. With twenty-four dents per inch in the reed, 16ˢ warp, three threads in a dent, and sixty picks per inch of 14ˢ weft, an excellent fabric will be obtained.

In fig. 97 a variation of the hunter's cord is given, known as the "Bedford." This is often produced in woollen and worsted. It differs in its construction from the modern ladies' dress-cloth which has usurped its name. It is made on ten shafts, with a thirty-six end draft, given in B, and six picks to the round. Good useful cloths are made in it by using a 30ˢ reed, with three, five, and six threads per dent, and 29 inches wide.

A great variety of weft and warp cords might be brought forward, but the principal having been given they will suffice for the purpose, as it is not difficult to produce others by changes of material, weaves, and drafting.

COTTON WEAVING.

Plush is a pile fabric having a longer pile than velvet or velveteen It is of two kinds, warp and weft plush. The former is made by the same means as silk velvet, cut-pile carpets, etc. The pile is formed by the insertion of wires, and cut by their withdrawal. The loop plushes, of which the familiar Brussels carpet is a type, are made in the same way, but the pile is not cut, as the wires are not armed with knives. Weft plush is made by merely extending the length of the pile of velvets and velveteens. It is made by the same weaves. The ground may be either plain or twilled. When woven it is cut in the same manner as velvets and cords, and dyed and finished as they are.

In making these goods it is best to use the sateen dis-

FIG. 98.   FIG. 99.

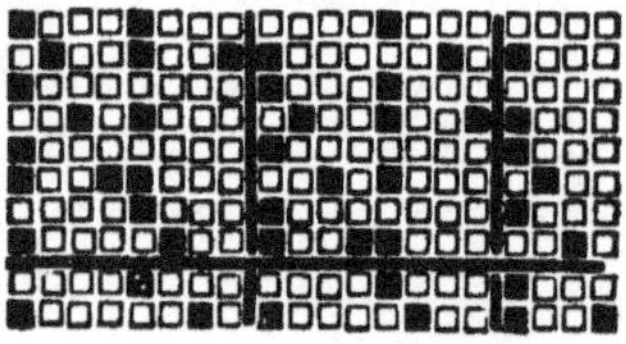

VELVETS, VELVETEENS, CORDS, AND PLUSHES (*continued*).

tribution of the stitching or binding threads, as regular courses are thus ensured for the cutter's knives. Fig. 98 gives a plush on eight shafts with a straight draft, two weft picks, plain weave for binders to form the back, and eight plush picks.

Fig. 99 is one on ten shafts, straight draft, and twenty picks to the round, five of which are used to form the twill back.

For seal or other imitation skins, fancy coloured mottled yarns are used, and, if necessary, a greater number of shafts with more extended drafts are brought into use, but the principles of construction are the same throughout, and this being the case further examples need not be given.

WOVEN FABRICS.

Gauze or Leno Fabrics.

We now come to the exposition of a weave which differs in its principle from any that have gone before, and constitutes the fabrics into which it is introduced, a class by themselves. In all the preceding weaves, however intricate the patterns are or may be made, one principle underlies them all; the warp and weft threads are arranged in their respective parallel orders, and more or less close together, according to the required density or openness of the fabric to be constructed. This order is also maintained in gauze or leno weaving, two names which are indifferently used to designate the same thing. The point of difference arises in the manner in which the intersections of the threads are made. Instead of the intersections being, as before, between the warp and weft threads, they are made entirely between the warp threads themselves, and bound in position by the weft threads. This is shown in the following illustration (fig. 100). There are two warp threads, A, B, and four weft threads shown. Let the student take the thread A, and examine its relationship to the weft. It will be found that it passes under every one of the four threads of weft. Now take the thread B, follow its course in the same way, and it will be found that it passes over every one of the four threads of weft. In all ordinary weaves with such an arrangement of warp and weft threads, there being no intersections between the two series of threads, there would be no fabric. The intersections, however, have been removed from the weft and transferred to the warp, and take place amongst the warp threads themselves, and only amongst them. It will be observed that the warp threads

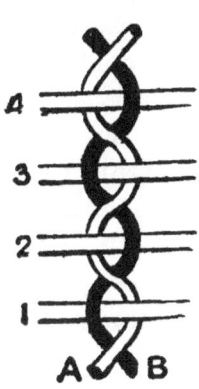

FIG. 100.

cross one another in the spaces from right to left, and left to right alternately. But even here they are not like the intersections of the ordinary weave: in making these crossings they never go under and over each other, as do the threads of warp under and over the threads of weft. They simply cross one another from side to side, the same threads being always uppermost and always undermost throughout their respective courses. It will be obvious that mere crossings of this kind could never make an arrangement of threads that would be permanent, which is an essential requirement in the construction of a woven fabric. Steps must therefore be taken to render these crossings of the warp threads permanent. This is accomplished by the introduction of the weft threads in the manner shown. In the shedding arrangement the white thread, A, is so actuated that it is depressed first on the right of the black thread, B, and then on the left of it, so much as to allow the weft threads, 1, 2, 3, 4, etc., always to pass over it. Correspondingly, the black thread, B, is always raised to let the weft threads pass under it, it thus coming to pass that the white thread is always down and the black thread always up in their final disposition. The function of the weft, it will thus be seen, is to form a binder or retaining thread, in order to keep the warp threads permanently in the position they have been made to assume. This passage of the warp threads across and partially around each other, is ordinarily described as a twisting movement, but this is not correct. The twist or twine is mostly imperfect, as only in a few special cases in the loom do the threads make a passage around each other of more than three-quarters of a revolution, from which point they reverse their movement, returning on the track they came to the point whence they started. In the lace machine or loom the revolution is complete, but it is made by the weft passing completely around a warp thread, instead of the partial twist of two warp threads.

The method of constructing gauze weaves differs con-

WOVEN FABRICS.

siderably from that of ordinary weaves, because of certain conditions governing the twisting of the warp threads. A design for gauze is therefore more difficult to comprehend, and before attempting to construct one, it will be desirable to briefly examine the mechanical devices for crossing the warp threads. Without the acquisition of this knowledge as a preliminary, it would be wasted time investigating the construction of gauze fabrics.

In weaving gauze fabrics, or seeking to introduce gauze effects amongst other weaves, two sets of heald shafts are required. The first set, called the plain shafts, *a*, is to produce the ordinary weave that may be required, and to co-operate with the gauze or second set, which are termed the gauze healds. The second set, for the crossing or twisting operation, carry the "doup" healds, *b*. Sometimes these are made with the doup shaft at the top and sometimes at the bottom; both these methods are shown in fig. 101. They have what weavers term a double eye, or an eye or opening for receiving the warp thread below the centre of the heald, and a second one immediately above. This set of healds or doups in working are always subject to a far larger amount of friction than the ordinary healds, and therefore require to be made of material that will successfully resist the great friction to which they are subject. This should be silk, or a strong and highly finished cord that has surfaces that will permit the warp threads to glide against them with a minimum of friction, and consequently of wear and tear. The two sets of shafts are, however, connected with each other by their healds, and therefore are actually arranged in pairs. Fig. 101 gives a good illustration of the construction of the doup heald. The loop, *e*, formed by the cord, passes through the eye of

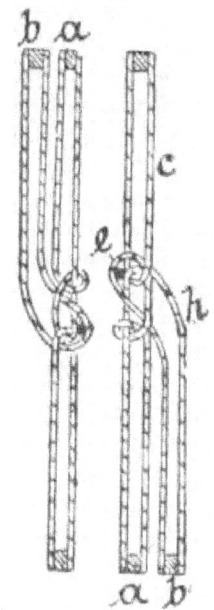

FIG. 101.

COTTON WEAVING.

the standard heald and carries a warp thread. This it transfers, in alternation, first to one side and then the other of its companion thread in the "standard" heald which holds the doup heald. This doup, with its thread, is the chief factor in gauze weaving. The doup cord is shown at *h*, and *c* is the standard heald.

In draughting or drawing in the warp, in cases where doup healds are employed, the first warp thread is drawn in the first shaft of the standard healds, as usual in plain cloth weaving, and then through its doup, whilst the next is drawn through the second standard shaft directly over the doup thread just described, both threads entering one

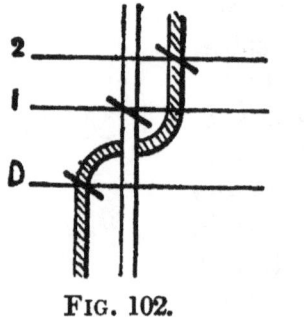

FIG. 102.

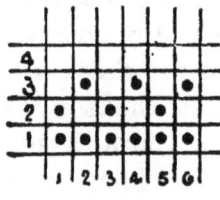

FIG. 103.

dent of the reed. And so the draft proceeds in this order across the warp. When the draft is decided upon, the drawing-in follows it as given.

In fig. 102, which is the pegging plan, D is the doup, and figs. 1, 2, the plain weave shafts. Fig. 104 shows the first thread on the first shaft, and the second thread on the second shaft, and so continued over the two shafts. In this figure the doup thread is shown at A, and, as will be observed, is passed under the threads with which it will work, and through the loop of the doup heald. The thread B is only drawn in on the regular shaft, and passes through the gauze shaft between the doup healds, without being subjected to them in any way. An examination will show that the doup thread A, in the plain healds, is on the left of B; in the gauze healds it is on the right of B. When the threads are thus arranged, their action is always conjoined, and they are dented, or drawn through the reed into the same space together.

In fig. 103 the weave plan for an ordinary gauze is shown on design paper. Two of the vertical lines constitute a representation of fig. 102, but the representation has been extended to three repeats, in order to show its appearance more fully upon paper.

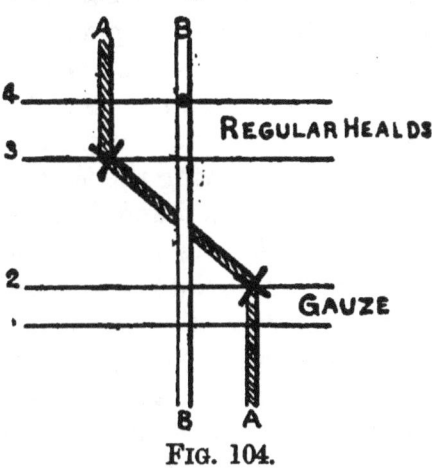

FIG. 104.

To give proper expression to the character of the gauze weave, it must have a contrasting plain or satin weave beside it in stripes, when it will stand out clearly and distinctly, forming a fine lace-like ornamentation. If it is desired to carry the ornamentation further, the fabric can be

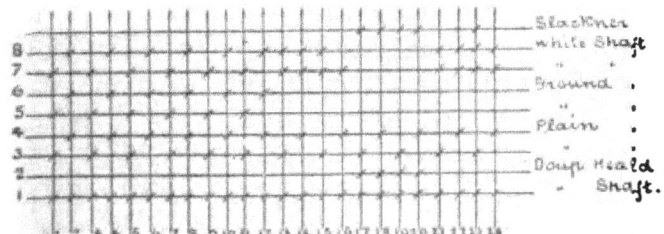

FIG. 105.

checked by a plain transverse stripe, in which case the weave must be of the same texture as the plain weave in longitudinal or plain warp stripe. The doup or whip-thread, or the ground, is double when gauze is made, but the plain weave separates them. Fig. 105 is the weave plan, numbered from 1 to 8. In this plan No. 1 gives the action of the doup shaft, which is raised at every weft pick; No. 2 is the doup heald, and it only rises with one on the four weft picks, 17, 18, 19, 20; the shafts 3 and 4 are for the plain stripe, and shafts 5 and 6 for the ground; these weave plain for twelve picks. Shafts 7 and 8 carry the doup or whip threads, which also weave plain for twelve picks. At the thirteenth pick they combine, and are up for four picks and down for four picks in alternation. During the time of this combined movement, the ground shafts 5 and 6 remain down. The ninth is the position of the slackening bar or rod, which has been introduced to obviate the necessity of employing two warp beams. It will be seen that it rises on the same picks as the doup healds, No. 2, whilst the whip shafts 7 and 8 are down; but the whip threads themselves are lifted to the opposite side of the ground threads, giving the twist or turn required. Of course the "reeding," that is, the drawing of the warp through the reed, of gauze or leno fabrics is specially considered in this case; twenty-four threads would be placed in eleven dents in the following order: four threads in the first dent, and the second dent vacant; again, four threads in the third dent, and another dent left vacant; four threads in the fourth dent, and two threads each in the next six dents. The word dent properly and primarily means tooth, and here indicates the teeth of the reed. It has, however, come to be used to designate the spaces between these teeth, and is so used above. The Scotch term of "splits" would be a more accurate one. The technical terms used in the textile industries, however, like those of nearly every other industry, require a thorough revision and clearer definition.

Very elaborate effects can be obtained with the use of gauze or leno healds, as the warp stripes and the checking can be varied to any desired extent by using a greater or less number of threads for either the plain or gauze effects.

If gauze fabrics are compared with any other cloth constructions, they will be found superior in lightness of texture and firmness of interlacing, which is due to the partial twist of the threads around one another, and the firm manner in which the weft secures them in that position, enabling the fabric to bear a great strain.

In reference to fig. 101, the draft and weave plan of which is given in fig. 102, if the weft picks are taken in their numerical order, it will be seen that the first raises the doup thread to the right, and the gauze shafts will be lifted, 1 and 2 being raised on this first weft pick. On the second pick the doup thread is transferred to the other side, and the shafts for this are the first and third. The shedding for the next pick is the same as the first; but the doup or skeleton shaft is always up, this being necessary for operating the doup thread by the action of either the ground shaft 2, or the gauze shaft 3. The fourth shaft is always down, as it carries a stationary thread, and may be regarded as an extra shaft only. In fig. 100 the warp threads are drawn so tightly to each other, that the weft pick cannot be drawn up very closely to the preceding pick, so that an open space is left between every pick, and vacant dents being left in the reed to correspond with these spaces, the gauze effect is the result.

The "warp-slackener" or "warp-easer" is a bar or rod which separates the crossing warp from the other. It is fixed at the back of the loom, and may be termed a lever. In the plain weave portion it is inactive; but when the crossing has to be made, a connection on the arm of this rod acts upon the doup heald, causing it to deliver sufficient warp to prevent injury to the other warp threads, after which it is drawn back to its former position by a spring. This method, however, is not suitable for more than the leno fabric in which the doup thread passes under one standard thread only, and in those in which the doup thread passes under more than one standard thread at a time it is necessary to adopt the old system of two beams, in order to diminish the strain upon the doup thread, and the friction upon the doup healds.

COTTON WEAVING.

The principles and methods thus laid down are generally followed throughout gauze weaving, any departure from them being mainly in the number of stationary threads, around which the doup threads twine, which may be increased as desired. Threads of different colours, or fancy stripes, may be produced to any extent, and gauze and figures, etc. All threads that work the same way can be drawn in on the one doup shaft. The jacquard machine and harness give an almost unlimited variety of figured gauzes; but the improvement in lace frames and their cheap productions, have caused the most elaborate forms of fancy woven gauzes to become an almost extinct branch of weaving.

Jacquard Harness.

In considering the weaves hitherto dealt with it will have been seen that the warp has always been mounted in what have been termed healds, themselves mounted upon and stretched between two staves of wood in number sufficient to meet requirements. A mount of healds of this kind is termed a leaf or shaft, and the number of these required to operate a warp are termed in turn a set of healds. As will be borne in mind, the simplest set is one of two leaves or shafts, advancing up to twenty or even twenty-five shafts; there are dobby machines will admit in extreme requirements up to forty shafts of healds, but the crowded state of the loom requires such a long stretch between the last heald shaft and back rest as to prevent their common use. Beyond these resort is had to the jacquard machine for shedding purposes, owing to its beautiful simplicity and great range of power. In the transition from the preceding system to the new one the terms hitherto used are dropped, and the set of healds becomes the jacquard harness. The simple construction of an ordinary harness is shown in fig. 106. The front now only is given. It will be seen to be composed of several parts: the first, the harness necks shown by the figures; the couplings shown at the knots, E E; the lingoes or weights, F. The harness necks are connected to the jacquard hooks by passing them through the bottom board of the machine upon which the hooks rest when not in action; these cords are also often termed neck bands. The couplings or knots, E E, shown above the comber board, are a continuation of the neck twines carrying the mails or eyelets, D, through which the warp threads pass, as in ordinary healds. The lingoes, or weights, upon each cord are for the purpose of bringing the warp threads down to their normal position after having been lifted by the hooks in accordance with the shedding requirements of the pattern.

Jacquard harness is full, half, or sometimes otherwise incomplete, according to the nature of the requirements in which it is used. The harness generally in use is the full harness, by which every warp thread throughout the tie if required can be operated singly and independently of the others. In a word it may be called the universal harness, capable of doing whatever can be accomplished by any other build or construction of jacquard mounting. Of course, as in heald shaft shedding arrangements, in the repeats of the pattern the corresponding threads are lifted simultaneously.

There are, as might be anticipated, many varieties of jacquard harness, such as the half, the gauze, the double cloth, the pressure, etc. The half harness has every alternate warp thread drawn in through the mail eye, the other threads only pass through the doups and standard or shaft healds in front of the comber board. This arrangement is used for obtaining a certain class of gauze effects or fabrics. The pressure harness has a given number of warp threads drawn in through each mail eye, which are also operated by heald shafts in order to weave the ground of the fabric. This is no doubt a useful and economical method of forming figures in cloth and saving cards, but it has very serious drawbacks owing to the excessive friction it entails upon the yarn in shedding.

COTTON WEAVING.

There are two plans of mounting a jacquard on the loom, both suitable for any tie or fabric. These are respectively called the London and Norwich systems, and both have their advocates. The London system arranges the jacquard at right angles with the harness; the Norwich one parallel with it. Our illustrations show the latter arrangement. Fig. 106 shows the front row of a jacquard harness. The horizontal lines A proceed to and are attached to the jacquard machine hooks; B shows the tail cords; C points out the knots connecting the upper and lower portion of the harness; D is the comber board; E the mail eyes through which the warp threads pass, and by which they are lifted to form a shed; and F, the lingoes, or weights, which draw the mails down to their normal position. In fig. 106 only the front row of the cords passing through the comber board D are shown, it not being necessary to exhibit more as all are alike. Now if in mounting the jacquard machine on the loom it be placed with its end to the front or at a right angle to the harness, the mount will be what is called the London plan, which twists the harness cords a half turn around each other. A moment's consideration will show how this happens, for whether the first cord is taken up from the front right or left-hand hole in the comber board, and secured to the front or back hooks of the jacquard machine the cords must eventually cross each other, and the constant rubbing which results in passing each other in forming every shed for the passage of the shuttle must be destructive to the cords. It is said by the admirers and advocates of this arrangement that the half twist it gives to the harness keeps the cords better within bounds, and that a heck or guide can be dispensed with. In the Norwich system the jacquard machine is arranged on the loom parallel with the harness, reed, and cloth, the strands or cords are taken up to the hooks just in the same order as a heald shaft with its complement of warp threads, and when a cord breaks it can be traced at once by separating the entire row from the next one, which can be done without the slightest difficulty, each row being entire and clear of each other. This is a very useful feature, greatly facilitating such repairs when needed.

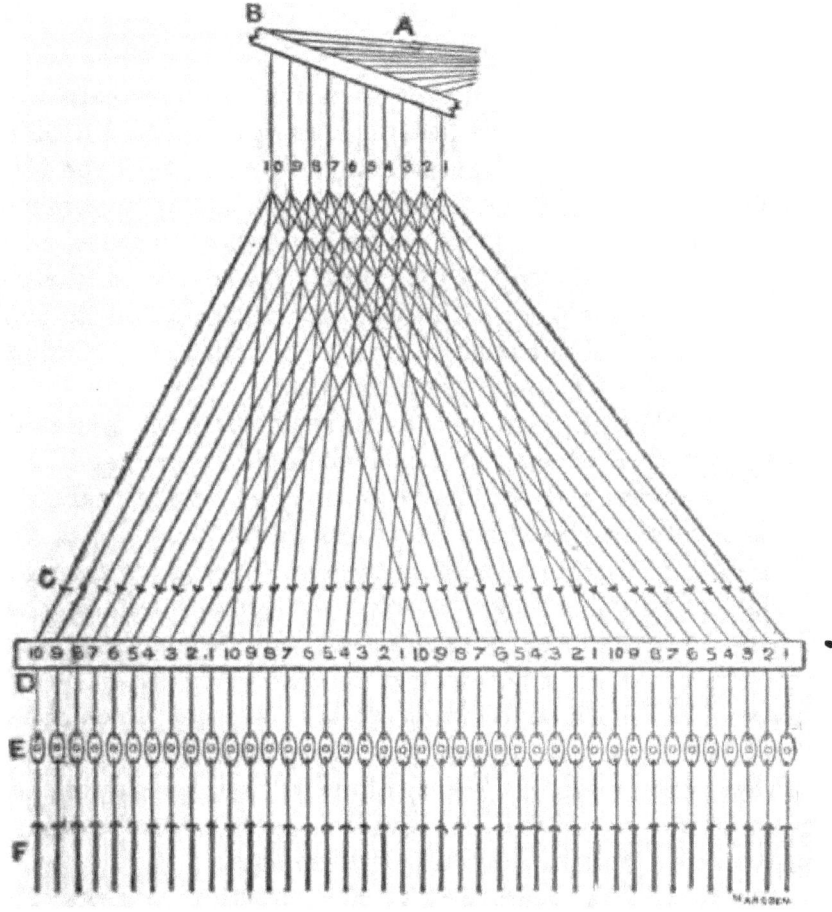

FIG. 106.—JACQUARD HARNESS, FRONT ROW ONLY.

A 400-hook jacquard really contains 408 hooks, the eight beyond the nominal count being allowed for the formation of the selvages of the cloth or other purposes. The 400 hooks are available for operating the warp threads in the production of the pattern across the field of the cloth to be made. They are, in their ultimate power, equivalent to 400 shafts of healds, as described in the exposition of shaft work, as this number of shafts would be required to produce the same capacity and extent of ornamentation.

The designer who has only 400-hook machines with which to work out his designs is limited by their capacity of work. To extend his designs he might require a 600, or two 400, two 600 machines, etc. In the case of the 400 machine, however, the comber board and the arrangement of the hooks may be taken to be eight holes across, and fifty holes in its length, with every harness cord direct from the mails through the comber board and on to the hooks in the machine, without crossing or chance of coming into contact and causing friction.

The number of holes in the comber board are regulated by the number of threads per inch in the warp, and the function of the comber board is to prevent the harness cords becoming entangled, and to maintain such an orderly arrangement amongst them as to permit of easy working; in fact, the comber board is simply a comb, combing the constantly moving harness cords into order, and from this function it has no doubt derived its name. Irrespective of any peculiar methods of tying up the harness, the comber board is divided into as many sections, or groups of holes, as there are hooks in the machine, though it may be so finely perforated that, as in healds, a given number may need to be left blank to meet requirements.

The ordinary method and the most practical and best in constructing the harness, is to take the tail of the first hook in the machine, and put a cord from it through the first division in the comber board, following with the second and succeeding hooks in a similar manner until all the hooks in the machine have as many cords attached to them as there are divisions in the board. Each of these divisions begins with a complete row, which must always be as fine as the warp reed. The form of the harness will

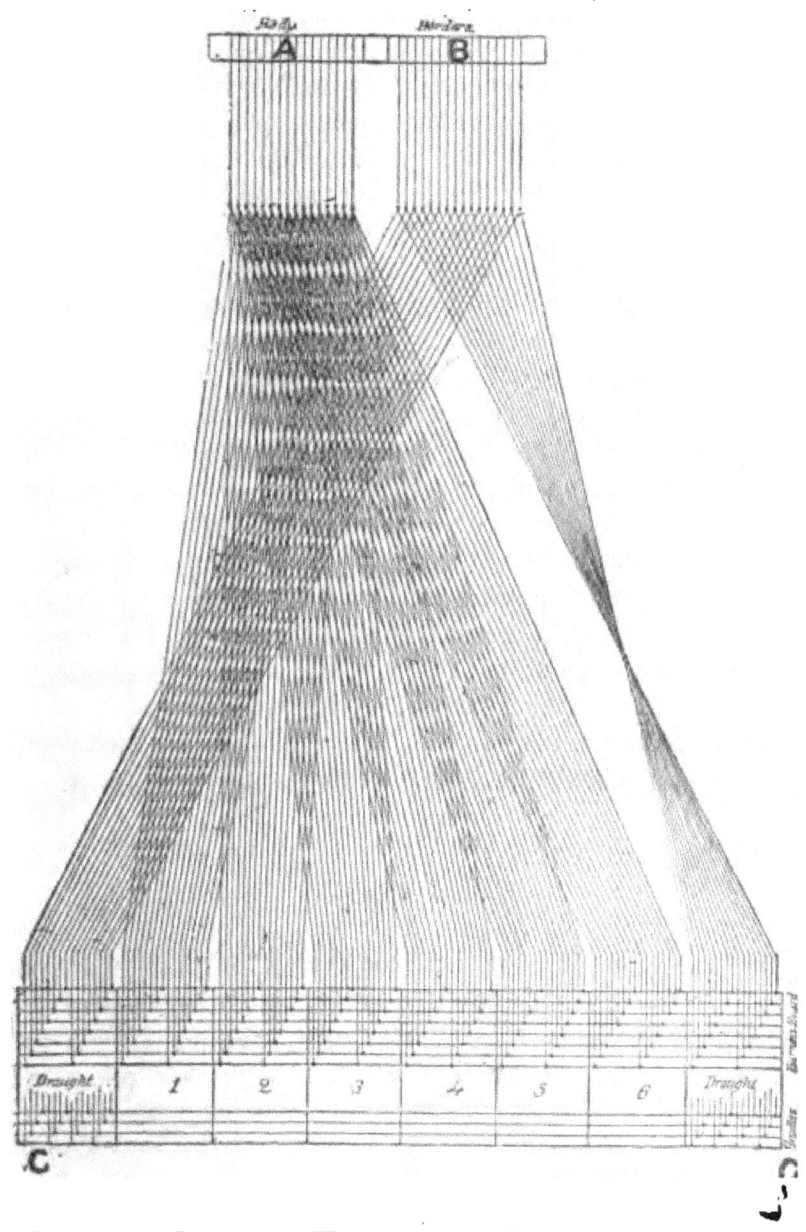

Fig. 107.—Jacquard Harness for Handkerchiefs or Bordered Cloths. Norwich System.

always depend, to a great extent, upon the particular fabric and style required, such as dress goods, double cloths, table-covers, bordered cloths, handkerchiefs, etc.

In fig. 107 is shown the "tie-up," "tie," or harness for a handkerchief, or bordered cloth of any kind, with full drafts and the position of the healds used to work the ground. The twist of the harness cords on the right-hand border is to prevent a reversal of the draft on this border, which would have to be made were it required that the harness should present the same appearance to the observer as it does on the opposite side. By this arrangement the inside of each border presents itself to the centre, or body, of the cloth. A careful study of the illustration (fig. 107) will clearly reveal this to the reader. It shows the body harness at A for weaving the central design of the fabric; the border harness at B and at C and C' shafts for weaving a plain or twill ground.

It is a common practice to build a harness with such a tie as will admit of a great variety of patterns for several classes of fabrics, and then to get the designer to work, if possible, within their capacity. Of course this is from an economical consideration, a motive which though very praiseworthy should not always have absolute control.

Damask Weaving.

In the preceding sections of this chapter, the power accruing to the textile fabric designer from increasing the number of his heald shafts has been shown. It was not deemed necessary to carry the exposition beyond a ten shaft set of healds, as the student who has mastered the details up to that point can easily travel to the boundary of shaft work himself. Also it may be remarked that every further addition to the number of shafts increases the cumbrousness of the system, and with all the necessary complement of shedding mechanism takes up so much space that an alternative method soon becomes highly desirable. This is found in the jacquard machine, a wonderful invention of the early part of the present century, of which a description will be given subsequently. This machine, as observed in a preceding page, practically gives the designer perfect control over the actuation of every thread in his warp, so that he can shed it independently of any other thread should he so desire, or the exigencies of his design require it. The great advantage thus resulting for the production of ornamental designs will be obvious at once.

It is in the production of the large floriated designs of damask fabrics that the designer is soon carried beyond the range of shaft work. When designs are wanted that pass beyond the scope of the latter, the sketch must be regulated by the nature of the texture required, and the size of the jacquard machines at command. Let it be assumed that a design is suitable for a 400-hook machine, and that the fabric must contain eighty warp threads per inch, by making 80 the divisor of 400 a quotient of 5 inches is arrived at, which gives the width of cloth available for one pattern. The length of the pattern depends upon the number of picks put into it, and may run to a great length. The number of picks to the round is governed by the pattern cards.

In the preparation of an original design, it is always best to make two or three repeats both in the warp and weft threads, as then, should the design prove weak in any respect, or fail to join in a satisfactory manner, the fault is easily discovered and remedied. The ornamental figures with which it is the object of the designer to decorate the fabric should, if possible, be so distributed upon the surface as to avoid the production of parallel, diagonal, or transverse rows. This can best be attained by the use of a weft sateen, or warp satin arrangement.

When it is necessary to transfer a sketch to point paper, the sketch is ruled or lined in squares to correspond with the paper, so that it can be enlarged very accurately. If a pattern is required to be copied from a fabric or drawing, then tracing paper must be used, which, placed upon a sheet of white paper, may be ruled in spaces as required. Suppose the sketch has been drawn upon point paper to appear as a cloth with sixty threads per inch, the same as the sketch, then the figure ornament must be enclosed in a square, and if it measures ·75, or three-quarters of an inch in length, and ·5 or half an inch in width, there will be in it forty-five weft threads or picks, and thirty warp threads in the entire pattern. Those who do not find it easy to rule a sketch in this manner, will find point paper a very reliable guide. Now to take this sketch upon the commonest type

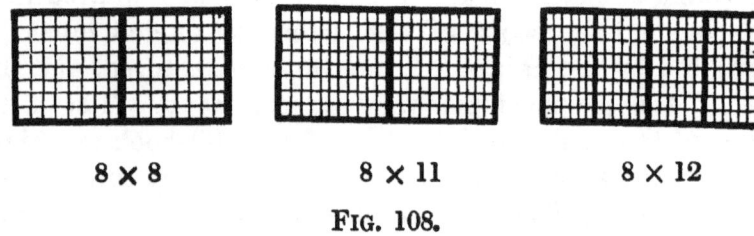

8 × 8   8 × 11   8 × 12

FIG. 108.

of point paper in use, 8 × 8 in one division—that is eight threads of warp and eight threads of weft in one of the large squares, the pattern would fill five large squares, and have five picks over in the weft way, the latter, of course, running into another square; and three large squares with six threads over in the warp way, the latter, like the weft picks, running into another large square to complete. An exact size of the sketch is thus reproduced.

Of design or point paper there are many types. Three are shown in fig. 108. It will be seen that they vary in the number of lines for weft threads. Let it be supposed that it is required to put upon paper a design containing 80 warp threads and 120 weft threads per inch, the design paper would require to be 8 × 12;

if 100 weft threads, 8 × 10, and so on in proportion. Should a 5 × 5 design be required for a fabric, 80 warp threads by 120 weft threads, the sketch would have to be enlarged so as to cover 400 warp and 600 weft threads; that is, 80 × 5 = 400, and 120 × 5 = 600, which would all be represented by the squares. The

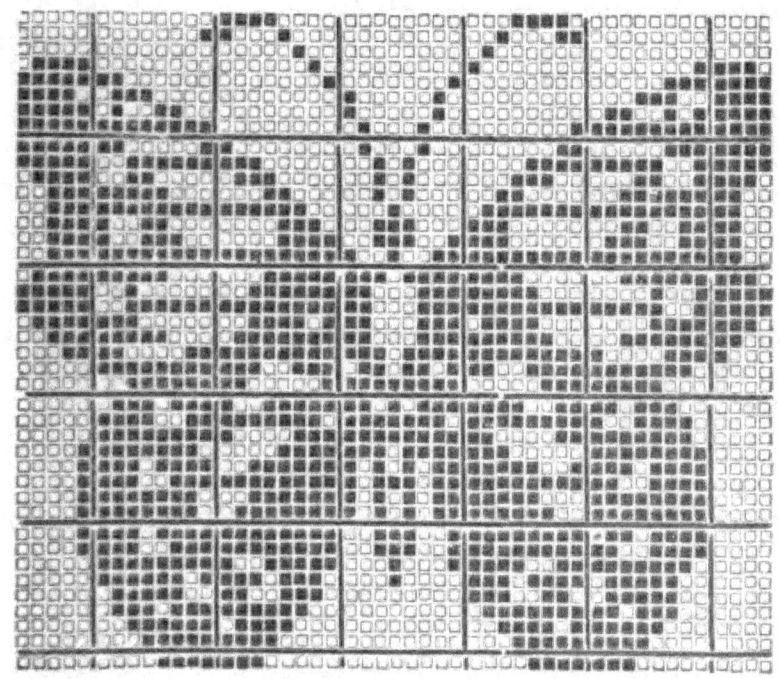

BUTTERFLY DESIGN.

FIG. 109.

simplest method of procedure, however, taking this as an illustration, would be to rule off on ordinary paper, 8 × 8, 400 × 600 squares, and trace the design by impression. Take, for example, the figure of the butterfly (fig. 109), which was drawn direct upon point paper. If required for a stripe, it could be produced on a dobby by a V-draft, without alteration of the figure, and with a plain ground intersecting its recurrence for a few picks. In such a reproduction twenty-five heald shafts would suffice for the figure, and four for the ground weave. But this design has been constructed for an "all-over" effect on a satin ground, each figure to be placed in position by a satin arrangement. Space, however, will hardly permit an extended description of this illustration; it must, therefore, suffice to say that the ground and figure must be a measure of each other. An examination will show that the figure covers forty-nine threads from left to right, so if a seven-shaft satin be taken for the ground, $7 \times 7 = 49$ shows the ground and figure with this would be in unison, and the joinings would be effected without a break. In its length, or weft-way, the design covers forty-one squares or picks, and as the figures require to be separated from each other, if eight satin picks are added thereto for this purpose, forty-nine, or the same number of threads as in the warp would be used, the ground and figure thus measuring alike.

In jacquard harness there are no complex drafts, all are straight over. The pattern or design must, if possible, cover a number of threads that will be a multiple of the number of hooks in the machine. If this cannot be done, what is termed casting-out must be resorted to. This means that a given number of jacquard hooks must be thrown out of action all the time. Thus, to revert to the butterfly illustration, it has been seen that forty-nine threads cover the figure. If this was made upon a 200-hook machine, four repeats would occur, with four of a remainder, thus $200 \div 49 = 4 + 4$. These four hooks would have to remain out of work all through the width and all through the length of the warp. The same thing occurs in all cases in which the threads in the design cannot be divided by the machine hooks without a remainder.

Besides the "casting-out" thus shown, a further necessity for resort to it arises, as in healds, owing to the exigencies of orders. The harness when built, whether on the London or Norwich principle, cannot be cut down and rebuilt to suit every change of density in the texture of warp threads per inch. It is always built to a certain proportion of threads per inch, and if a less number than this is required in a fabric, the unnecessary ones may be cast or left out in the drafting. But there is not the same liberty in the opposite direction: under no circumstances can any be added. This being the case, and the reed being a controlling factor, it becomes merely an arithmetical calculation under the rule of proportion. Take, as an illustration, the case of a harness tied up to weave ninety threads per inch, but the order in hand is for a fabric to contain eighty-six threads per inch. Therefore if the jacquard machine is a 400-hook, the problem stands as follows: As $90 : 400 :: 86 = 382$. Subtracting 382 from 400, there are 18 left, which is the number of mails in the harness, holes in the comber board, and hooks in the jacquard that will require to be left vacant. These remarks will be sufficient to show how design figures and lower reeds may be adapted to the capacity of the harness and jacquard machines, however many hooks they may have from 100 upwards.

The Analysis or Dissection of Woven Fabrics.

It often happens in actual practice that manufacturers have samples or patterns of cloth submitted to them for imitation, or "matching," as it is usually called. These often spring from some interruption of communications with the sources of the original supply, which may arise from many causes.

The points to be noted in order are, 1st, the dimensions, which simply mean width and length; 2nd, the substance, which implies weight of the warp, weft, and the sizing materials; 3rd, the quality of the yarns, and the composition and quality of the sizing materials; and 4th, the texture or weave. To ensure a satisfactory result all these points require careful examination, which can only be made by dissection, and from the knowledge thus gained accurate reconstruction on parallel lines will result by the use of proper care. It will not be enough for even the most clever experts to merely glance at a piece of cloth, count the warp and weft, and then proceed to make it from such meagre details, disappointment and dissatisfaction will almost surely result.

With the knowledge of cloth construction gained from the examples already given, in which it is traced from its simplest to moderately intricate forms, and their practical application shown, the dissection of samples will be found both simple and easy. In the simplest weaves a mere inspection of the fabric will suffice to reveal what the weave is, but in intricate patterns a much more careful procedure becomes necessary, and the following instructions should be carefully observed:—Take the sample of cloth, or a portion sufficiently large to contain an entire round and a small portion on each side. Draw from this several threads both of warp and weft, so as to leave a short fringe of both on their respective sides. This will facilitate the examination. Commence the operation by pushing back a weft thread (not pulling it out) from its position near the other still in its place. Proceed to count the intersections this pick makes with the warp threads from the right to the left. In taking out the pick all the threads of the warp which the weft passes over must be marked in their regular order on the point paper until a repeat occurs, which will be shown by the weft going over in the same order as before. In fig. 110 is given an illustration, with the warp and weft threads numbered. In relation to the first weft pick it will be observed

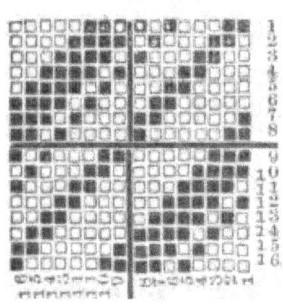

FIG. 110.

that the first two warp threads are down, three next up, one down, one up, four down, and five up. The first pick having been carefully taken out and registered, proceed as before from the same point. Here the first warp thread is up, next two down, three up, one down, one up, four down, and this is marked No. 2 on the point paper. The dissection is proceeded with in this manner until a pick is found, which repeats the positions of that first taken out and marked No. 1. Thus the round or repeat of the fabric in the weft way is found. The weave plan shows sixteen shafts or warp threads and sixteen picks of weft as the round, forming a fancy twill with the angle to the right, which is its proper inclination. The warp threads or shafts numbered show the draft to be straight over the healds, and as no two are alike this draft cannot be reduced. This illustration shows the whole process of dissection to be pursued in any weave, however complex it may be. The fringe of warp yarn will show the colour pattern, if any, and the weft pattern, if in colours, can be seen in the weft fringe. These colours and their order of succession must be written down in detail, for "costing," that is, ascertaining the cost of producing it, dyeing, warping, etc. The threads of warp and weft may be compared with well-known standard counts to discover their numbers, or better still, be accurately ascertained by means which will be found described elsewhere in these pages. If in the sample submitted for dissection the selvages are absent, the warp threads can usually be distinguished from the weft by being harder twisted, by the size upon them, and generally by being of coarser counts. Samples are sometimes dissected by taking out the warp threads and leaving in the weft picks.

We close this section with an illustration, fig. 111, of the manner in which the simple weaves that have been expounded in this chapter can be utilized for the production of variegated effects suitable for many purposes. The example given is an extract from the "Textile Mercury" of December 9th, 1893. It is a rich and beautiful design, primarily for ladies' dress goods, but suitable for many other purposes. It is a combination of the powers of the four-shaft twill, and besides being of practical value to the manufacturer as given, constitutes an exceedingly

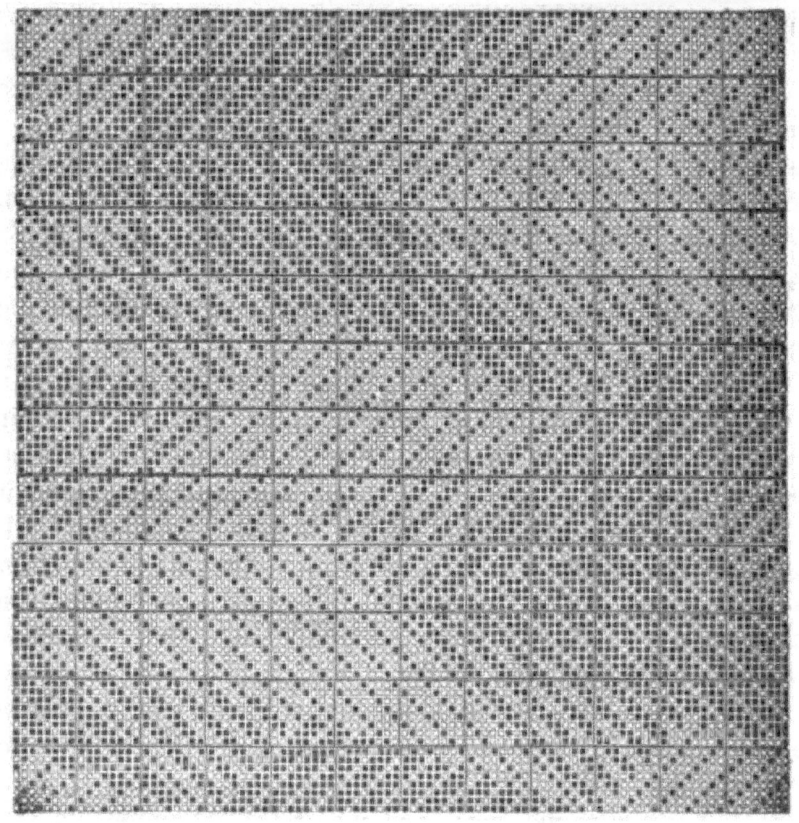

FIG. 111.—DESIGN FOR LADIES' DRESS GOODS.

valuable example to the textile student, offering an excellent study full of suggestiveness as to what may be accomplished on the same lines with other twills. If the powers of a higher twill had been employed the permutations would have become enormously greater and richer. The design as given, however, would look exceedingly well in

WOVEN FABRICS.

many classes of fabrics besides dress goods, and in many materials. The exigencies of page space have compelled the reduction of the design to rather small dimensions, but it is sufficiently clear to answer all requirements, whilst it gives a nearer approximation to its actual effect in a woven fabric than if set in larger type.

www.ingramcontent.com/pod-product-compliance
Lightning Source LLC
Chambersburg PA
CBHW031322150426
43191CB00005B/299